Christ for the World

KINGSWOOD BOOKS

Rex D. Matthews, Director
Candler School of Theology

EDITORIAL ADVISORY BOARD

W. Stephen Gunter
Candler School of Theology

Richard P. Heitzenrater
The Divinity School, Duke University

Thomas A. Langford
The Divinity School, Duke University

Robin W. Lovin
Perkins School of Theology

Mary Elizabeth Mullino Moore
School of Theology at Claremont

Jean Miller Schmidt
Iliff School of Theology

Neil M. Alexander, *ex officio*
Abingdon Press

Christ for the World

United Methodist Bishops Speak on Evangelism

Edited by
James C. Logan

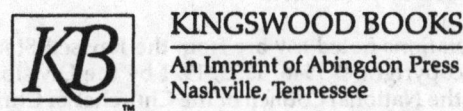

KINGSWOOD BOOKS
An Imprint of Abingdon Press
Nashville, Tennessee

CHRIST FOR THE WORLD:
UNITED METHODIST BISHOPS SPEAK ON EVANGELISM

Copyright © 1996 by Abingdon Press
All Rights Reserved

No part of this work may be reproduced or transmitted in any form or by any means, electronic or mechanical, including photocopying and recording, or by means of any information storage or retrieval system, except as may be expressly permitted by the 1976 Copyright Act or in writing from the publisher. Requests for permission should be addressed in writing to Abingdon Press, 201 Eighth Avenue, South, Nashville, TN 37203, USA.

Library of Congress Cataloging-in-Publication Data

Christ for the world: United Methodist bishops speak on evangelism / edited by James C. Logan.
   p.   cm.
   Contains edited versions of the major presentations made to the second Consultation on Theology and Evangelism, sponsored by the Foundation for Evangelism, held in Oxnam Chapel at Wesley Theological Seminary, Washington, DC, Mar. 9-12, 1995.
   Includes bibliographical references.
   ISBN 0-687-02206-1 (alk. paper)
   1. Evangelistic work—Congresses.   2. United Methodist Church (U.S.)—Membership—Congresses.   3. Methodist Church—United States—Membership—Congresses.   I. Logan, James C.
   BV3755.C48   1996
   269'.02'08827—dc20   95-48486
                                                                    CIP

Unless otherwise noted, all Scripture quotations are from the New Revised Standard Version Bible, copyright © 1989 by the Division of Christian Education of the National Council of the Churches of Christ in the USA. Used by permission.

Scripture quotations noted RSV are from the Revised Standard Version of the Bible, copyright © 1946, 1952, 1971 by the Division of Christian Education of the National Council of the Churches of Christ in the USA. Used by permission.

This book is printed on acid-free, recycled paper.

96 97 98 99 00 01 02 03 04 05 — 10 9 8 7 6 5 4 3 2

MANUFACTURED IN THE UNITED STATES OF AMERICA

Contents

Preface 7
Introduction 11
    PART ONE: FOUNDATIONS 17

Chapter 1: Biblical Faith and Evangelism
Neil L. Irons 19

Chapter 2: Evangelism in a Wesleyan Perspective
R. Sheldon Duecker 33

Chapter 3: Evangelism in the Otterbein-Albright Tradition
George W. Bashore 47

    PART TWO: CHURCH 57

Chapter 4: Evangelism by All God's People
Ann B. Sherer 59

Chapter 5: The United Methodist Church as Evangelist
Richard B. Wilke 69

Chapter 6: Discipleship and the Evangelistic Task
Bruce P. Blake 81

PART THREE: FRONTIERS 91

Chapter 7: Multicultural Evangelism
Hae-Jong Kim 93

Chapter 8: Multicultural Evangelism: A Response
    from a Hispanic American Perspective
Elias G. Galvan 105

Chapter 9: Evangelism and Secularization
Ruediger R. Minor 111

Chapter 10: Evangelism in the Marketplace
Woodie W. White 123

Chapter 11: Intellectual Challenges to the Gospel
Kenneth L. Carder 133

Chapter 12: The Global Gospel
Alfred L. Norris 143

Chapter 13: The Global Gospel: A Response
    from an African Perspective
Arthur F. Kulah 153

Appendix: "God's Gracious Love Affair":
    A Sermon on Isaiah 43:1-4
Joseph H. Yeakel 159

Contributors 165

Respondents 166

Abbreviations 167

Notes 167

Preface

"I HAVE NEVER SEEN as many bishops of the church assembled in one place except at General Conference or when the Council of Bishops has been in session!" This was the comment of one church official attending the second Consultation on Theology and Evangelism sponsored by The Foundation for Evangelism and held in Oxnam Chapel at Wesley Theological Seminary, Washington, DC, March 9–12, 1995. From my own knowledge of the activities of the Council across 31 years as a member, I would certify the accuracy of this observation, and offer one additional comment. I believe the Washington Consultation was the only occasion during my lifetime when the episcopal leadership of our denomination has been afforded a forum to deal exclusively with the theme of Christian evangelism.

The subject of this second Consultation was "Christ for the World; Evangelism in the Contemporary Church and World; Bishops of The United Methodist Church Speak." The detailed preparation for this event was guided by Dr. James C. Logan, E. Stanley Jones Professor of Evangelism at Wesley Theological Seminary and contributing editor of this volume. Dr. Logan performed a similar service for the first Consultation held at Emory University, Atlanta, Georgia, in 1992, and edited the anthology featuring essays from that event (*Theology and Evangelism in the Wesleyan Heritage* [Nashville: Kingswood Books, 1994]). In addition to the nineteen bishops present for the 1995 program, other distinguished denominational leaders attended and played important roles during the sessions held in our nation's capital. Among these were Mrs. Betty Ann Boulton, organist and spouse of Bishop Boulton, who collaborated with her husband in the presentation of what proved to be memorable times of worship during the Consultation; Dr. W. Stephen Gunter, Arthur J. Moore Associate Professor of Evangelism, Candler School of Theology, Emory

University; Dr. William Holmes, Senior Pastor, Metropolitan Memorial United Methodist Church, Washington, DC, who permitted the closing session of the Consultation to be held in connection with the morning worship service at Metropolitan Memorial on Sunday, March 12; Dr. Carolyn E. Johnson, Director of African-American Studies at Purdue University and President of United Methodist Women, The United Methodist Church; Dr. Henry H. Knight III, E. Stanley Jones Professor of Evangelism, Saint Paul School of Theology; Dr. Robert J. Stamps, Senior Pastor, Clarendon United Methodist Church, Arlington, Virginia; Dr. K. James Stein, Jubilee Professor of Church History, Garrett-Evangelical Theological Seminary; Dr. Roger K. Swanson, Director of Evangelism Ministries, General Board of Discipleship; and Dr. Sondra Wheeler, Assistant Professor of Christian Ethics, Wesley Theological Seminary.

Others who contributed significantly to the second Consultation were the fifty-voice choir of the Korean United Methodist Church of Greater Washington, McLean, Virginia, The Reverend Dr. Young Jin Cho, minister, and Mr. Jin Seung Kim, director; and The Reverend Stephen A. Rhodes and other leaders of Culmore United Methodist Church, Falls Church, Virginia, whose experimental program in multicultural evangelism was featured at the Saturday evening banquet.

Because of their particular significance in relating evangelism to ethnic and international cultures, the perceptive responses of Bishop Elias Galvan and Bishop Arthur Kulah are included with the essays published herein. Although it was not possible to make their statements a part of this volume, it should be noted that two of the respondents, Bishop David J. Lawson and Bishop James K. Mathews, presented important papers related respectively to discussions on "Evangelism and Secularization" and "The Gospel and the Intellectual Challenge."

It cannot be said too emphatically that a principal purpose of The Foundation for Evangelism throughout the forty-six years of its existence, since it was founded by the late Dr. Harry Denman, Methodism's celebrated lay apostle, has been to provide a solid base of intellectual, biblical, and theological respectability for winning persons to Jesus Christ and the Christian life. This purpose is reflected in The Foundation's sponsorship and funding of Professorships of Evangelism in United Methodist seminaries in this country and others, and in the more basic achievement of status for evangelism as an academic discipline in theological curricula. The establishment of periodic symposia for discussion of evangelism in a scholarly setting constitutes another effort to restore the process of confronting the human mind and heart with the Christian evangel to a more elevated position in contemporary religious thought and mission. The first Consultation three years earlier assembled scholars of the Methodist world from four continents to deal with what proved to be essentially a theoretical approach to evangelism and its theology. The second Consultation was focused more upon the practical mission of the church in the United States, and elsewhere, in what some thinkers have called the postmodern era. The choice of bishops to deliver the major presentations was a deliberate one, based on the fact that, as leaders in United Methodism, they confront daily the enormous and often baffling task of helping the church obey its Great Commission and replenish in each generation its people resources. It would be fair to say that all who heard the major presentations in Washington (and there were many lay and clerical auditors) were impressed by the analytical and provocative quality of the papers presented. It is their substantive value that makes their publication in this volume both important and exciting.

As always, participants and visitors during the Consultation discovered an indebtedness to their hosts for gracious amenities that provided both comfort and convenience. The thoughtful and generous assistance given by Dr. G. Douglass Lewis, President of Wesley Theological Seminary; The Rev. David McAllister-Wilson, Executive Vice President; Ms. Joanne Rutledge, secretary for Institutional Advancement; Ms. Beth Cogswell, Food Services Director; and Pam and Dan Horner and Lisa McKee, seminary students, were all significant factors in the success of the sessions. As always, the creative planning and vigilant oversight of Professor Logan were indispensable parts of a nearly incredibly smooth operation. Officials and members of the staff of The Foundation for Evangelism, Paul R. Ervin, Jr., William M. Hubbard, and Mrs. Freida Rhinehart, together with Dr. and Mrs. William L. Apetz, Mr. and Mrs. Robert B. Carpenter, Jr., Mr. and Mrs. David M. Stanley, Dr. Alan K. Waltz, Dr. Roger K. Swanson, and Dr. and Mrs. Robert F. Lundy, worked indefatigably to make our highest visions for this event materialize.

Important basic financial support for the project was provided by two trustee families, Mr. and Mrs. Phillip F. Connolly and Mr. and Mrs. David Stanley, and by one friend of The Foundation for Evangelism, Mrs. Lois P. Bowie. The presence throughout the sessions of Mr. Neil M. Alexander, Book Editor of The United Methodist Church, was an inspiration. Special gratitude needs to be expressed to Dr. Robert K. Feaster, President and Publisher of the United Methodist Publishing House, Mr. Alexander, and Dr. Rex D. Matthews, Senior Editor of Academic Books for Abingdon Press, all of whom have been instrumental in providing the program of this Consultation with the permanence of the printed page.

Very special gratitude should be expressed to all the presenters and respondents who spoke during the Consultation. Although their expenses were borne by The Foundation, no one expected or received an honorarium.

The second Consultation was a carefully conceived effort to focus the spiritual and intellectual attention and energy of United Methodism on the evangelistic task as a new century approaches. Born in the mind of one of our regional directors, The Reverend Ralph E. Bauserman, the entire undertaking represented a deep conviction on the part of Foundation trustees that a strong episcopal voice on the subject of winning persons to Christ can prove effective and influential in evoking a renaissance of evangelistic fervor for these times of deep trouble and exciting opportunities.

So may it prove to be!

Earl G. Hunt, Jr.

Introduction

THE YEAR WAS 1744. John Wesley convened his preachers for what was to become an annual "conferring." This was, in fact, the first Methodist Conference. On this occasion three questions were primary for consideration: "What to teach? How to teach? and What to do?" The Wesleyan Revival was struggling with what the church historically has called the *magisterium* or teaching office.

Today, the call for a recovery of the teaching office of the church is heard from various quarters. Voices do not speak with equal precision as to what the teaching office is (function) and where such an office is located (authority and structure). There is, nevertheless, general agreement that the people called United Methodists need a new sense of direction which is rooted in a renewed sense of identity.

In the early days of the American Methodist experiment the teaching office or function was exercised primarily by Bishops Asbury and Coke and mediated through itinerating preachers who served as mentors to others. In 1840 the Reverend E. S. James summarized this particular teaching method by comparing it with Jesus' teaching his disciples:

> I have never learned of any school for the education of ministers that so nearly resembled this as that of the itinerant ministry of the Methodist Church. . . . In this school, an aged and experienced minister, the best possible representative of Christ, takes a young man to travel and labor with him, as much as circumstances will allow, he directing his labors, and studies, and watching over his piety and conduct.[1]

The method of itinerant teaching was guided and informed by doctrinal tracts incorporated in the *Discipline*, a practice covering the period of 1788–1808. That the *Discipline* was a teaching tool is attested by the fact that from 1792 until 1964 the official title of the volume was *The Doctrines and Discipline*.

In the United Brethren and Evangelical traditions ordained elders exercised much the same pattern as did the Methodists in oversight and instruction. Without the explicit authoritative figure of one like Francis Asbury the itinerating preachers of these traditions nevertheless served likewise as the instructors and transmitters of the tradition.

The teaching office is more a *function* than a locatable *structure* in the traditions of The United Methodist Church. While these traditions have not been "confessional" in the sense of requiring clergy to subscribe to an official confession, the traditions have not been indifferent to matters of faith and practice. In any tradition the teaching office entails the functions of preservation, transmission, and interpretation of the faith. Without the exercise of these functions there is little possibility of gaining and maintaining a *sensus fidelium*. Many United Methodists are asking of their church no less than this.

♦ ♦ ♦

THE YEAR WAS 1995. Nineteen bishops of The United Methodist Church assembled in Washington, DC, March 9–12, 1995, for a Consultation on Theology and Evangelism, the theme of which was "Christ for the World." They were invited by The Foundation for Evangelism to address the pressing issue of "Evangelism in the Contemporary Church and World." In recent years the bishops of the church have been attempting to recover their share of the responsibility entailed in the teaching office. Most notable in recent times have been their "pastorals" on *In Defense of Creation* (1986)[2] and *Vital Congregations/Faithful Disciples* (1990).[3] The essays in this volume are not official statements of the Council of Bishops, but they represent, nonetheless, bishops of the church seeking to fulfill their responsibilities for "spiritual oversight" through teaching.

The essays in this volume derive from the major presentations and the concluding sermon of the Consultation. Limitations of space unfortunately preclude the inclusion of the contributions of most of the respondents. The responses of Bishop Elias G. Galvan and Bishop Arthur F. Kulah have been included because they vividly express specific perspectives within an inclusive world church. The Consultation was shaped and given context by the sensitive and creative worship led by Bishop and Mrs. Edwin C. Boulton. Excerpts from the worship precede each of the three major sections.

The Consultation was structured in a threefold plan seeking to focus upon the pressing needs of the contemporary church in its evangelism outreach. Reflecting that structure, the sections of this book are entitled Foundations, Church, and Frontiers. From the perspective of the needs of the church, they could also be characterized as Identity, Being, and Mission.

Foundations

Searching for a sense of identity necessarily involves the church in probing its roots or foundations. Bishop Neil L. Irons, speaking from a *Heilsgeschichte* or salvation history hermeneutic, unfolds the biblical narrative of God's salvific activity from creation through covenant to Christ and from Christ to church to consummation. He demonstrates that the biblical warrant for evangelism is not to be found in one or more selected texts but in and through the whole canonical text. Bishop R. Sheldon Duecker addresses our identity in the Wesleyan tradition by delineating the distinctive Wesleyan understanding of grace—prevenient, justifying, and sanctifying—and shows how this understanding of grace was structured in the Wesleyan revival in the societies and classes. The traditions of Otterbein and Albright are interpreted by Bishop George W. Bashore, who makes a significant contribution by exploring the content, meaning, and role played by the *Heidelberg Catechism* in the United Brethren tradition.

Church

While the church is not the objective of evangelism, it is certainly the means of evangelism. This is crucial for the traditions making up The United Methodist Church. These traditions were in mission before they ever became churches, and lodged in the very structures of the earliest days were the intuitions and convictions of figures such as Wesley, Asbury, Otterbein, and Albright that mission was not an appendage to the church but constituted the church's very *esse*. Bishop Ann B. Sherer explores the ministry of all baptized Christians, the *laos*, and offers guidelines for a contemporary practice of outreach evangelism. Bishop Richard B. Wilke follows with a call for the church to recover its pivotal role as the announcer or herald of the gospel. Making a distinction, but not separation, between evangelism and discipleship, Bishop Bruce P. Blake reflects upon the American church in the light of recent experiences with the church in Africa.

Frontiers

Obviously the ministry of evangelism faces innumerable frontiers today. Bishop Hae-Jong Kim, with roots in Korean Methodism and having been formerly the Director of the Multi-Ethnic Center for Ministry, brings his rich background to bear on the frontier of multicultural evangelism. Bishop Elias G. Galvan responds by reflecting upon evangelism in the Hispanic-American context. Bishop Ruediger R. Minor, having lived and ministered in East Germany and now located in Moscow, brings his analytical skills to center upon the phenomena of secularization and secularism as the context for evangelism. Formerly the General Secretary of the General Commission on Religion and Race, Bishop Woodie W. White considers evangelism in the marketplace of the poor, the marginalized, and the prosperous. Bishop Kenneth L. Carder presents an agenda for the church as it confronts the intellectual challenges rooted in the Enlightenment and post-Enlightenment eras, stressing the doctrines of Christology (the finality of Jesus Christ), eschatology (God's reign over creation), and ecclesiology (the search for Christian community). Bishop Alfred L. Norris, who chairs the section on evangelism in the General Board of Discipleship, brings the volume to a climax with an analysis of cross-cultural evangelism in a global perspective. Bishop Arthur F. Kulah responds from his engagement in Liberian Methodism and the All-Africa Conference of Churches.

The closing service of worship for the Consultation was celebrated in Metropolitan Memorial United Methodist Church with Bishop Joseph H. Yeakel as preacher. Bishop Yeakel's sermon on "God's Gracious Love Affair (Isaiah 43:1-4)" makes a fitting conclusion for the volume, as it did for the Consultation.

The bishops of the church here offer a cogent and passionate witness. The agenda for evangelism in the contemporary church and world is indeed a weighty one. The presentations recorded in this volume bear clear witness to this. In retrospect one is made conscious of yet unaddressed issues. Theologically one such pressing issue is the cross of Jesus Christ. P. T. Forsyth captured this imperative in an early twentieth-century work, *The Cruciality of the Cross*.[4] Indeed the cruciality of the atoning death of Jesus Christ is at the center of the church and its evangelistic ministry. No other issue is more critical for the church and its witness. Closely related is the matter of preaching. How do we effectively and faithfully witness to the cross in our time? Certainly all the contributions in this volume speak to these issues. Faith in the crucified Jesus and the preaching witness to this, the very center of Christian faith, cry out for more concentrated and specific attention. Consideration of these issues could be the making of a future Consultation.

Evidence that the church was listening to the bishops was manifested in the responses of those who attended the Consultation. Pastors, lay persons, seminary professors and students provided a "full house" to hear their episcopal leaders. The publication of this volume provides the opportunity for the whole church to read and listen. Again, our episcopal leadership has shown that it can speak forcefully; it remains to be seen whether the church can respond with equal vigor.

Gratitude should be expressed to Bishop Earl G. Hunt, Jr., and to the Board of The Foundation for Evangelism for the vision which guided and made possible this contribution to the church. Special appreciation should also be extended to the participating bishops who have made substantive efforts in their presentations and have courageously placed their manuscripts in my hands for the final editing. This was certainly a venture of faith on their part. I personally am greatly indebted to Ms. Veronica Boutté, who not only did all the secretarial work with thoroughness but was also a rich source of editorial guidance.

James C. Logan

PART ONE

Foundations

I AM BRINGING YOU good news of a great joy for all the people: to you is born this day in the city of David a Savior, who is the Messiah, the Lord.

Luke 2:10b-11

ONCE UPON A TIME, St. Matthew tells us, the events which swirled about Jesus must have made those who were his closest followers weary. They may—who knows?—in their heart of hearts have felt like another laborer in the vineyard well known to us. "I went to America to convert the Indians, but, oh, who shall convert me?" Is there a balm for the weary vinedresser, and refreshment for the laborer who needs saving?

Bishop Edwin C. Boulton

IT'S A PITY that we nearly always seek the salvation of Christ and his death outside of ourselves. . . . To experience the death of Jesus is more than hearing or telling about it.

Philip William Otterbein

CHAPTER 1

Biblical Faith and Evangelism

Neil L. Irons

BIBLICAL FAITH is expressed in the written word of Scripture, is conveyed through an unbroken living tradition which has God as its object, is lived out in a community of the faithful, and addresses all the world with saving, gracious love. Centered in the Word, biblical faith affirms that God speaks to humankind and that we can hear. Not only can we hear, but we are privileged to witness the actions of God within the realm of this world and to recognize them as such, whether they be actions of salvation or judgment. The Word of God, whether it be delivered by a prophet such as Isaiah or be present in the Incarnation of Jesus Christ, brings about its intended result within the human community. Even nations are unable to halt the mission of the Word truly sent by God. This is unqualified good news indeed.

The experience of the numinous was, and is, widespread in the world. For Israel, and later for those in Christ, this was also true. One thinks of Moses and the burning bush, Isaiah's vision in the temple, Ezekiel's feverish dreams, the Transfiguration of Jesus, Paul on the road to Damascus, and St. John on Patmos. But what is startling and promising is the confidence of the faithful that it is the presence of the divine Word—not the experience of the numinous—through which liberating, saving redemption occurs. No one, neither pharaoh nor Herod, can escape the ways of the Lord. The rule of God is ultimately superior to any human force, especially armies or principalities under the sway of demonic forces. And the faithful report these activities of God within history, and take assurance in them.

Biblical faith calls believers to the "good news" truth about what God has done, is doing, and will do. This gospel activity, which we call evangelism, points to the continuing movement of God toward "us," the whole human family. The whole of creation, including this planet, receives the Holy Presence which can be known and experienced, according to the biblical revelation. This revelation tells the world that shalom, peace, justice, salvation, and life are the divine intentions for all, and that God has the power to bring them to pass.

Originally, the term *evangel* was used to refer to the oral reporting of good news, as Furnish reminds us.[1] This general usage came over into the Bible, primarily, at the hands of Paul who used the term in reference to the Jesus-event, God's own powerful saving presence and activity. This is its central meaning in the New Testament.

Although the word *evangel* is rare in the Old Testament, it is no great stretch of the imagination to recognize that all biblical theology is built around powerful events in which God came to save those in desperate need. Therefore, remembering those times when a good word came from on high to deliver people from incredibly painful, faith-challenging events is essential to the task of this paper. In remembering, the first step of evangelism occurs.

The Old Testament

The beginning of the gospel is to be found in the opening fanfare of scripture located in Genesis 1:1–2:4a. These verses alert the reader to the fact that the Old Testament is a rich source of incredible hope. Any reflection on the theme of "Biblical Faith and Evangelism" starts here.

God created the heavens and the earth (Gen. 1:1). By divine speech, God calls the world into being. Simultaneously, Elohim (God) imbues the creation with meaning. It is good. When the creation of humanity, male and female, occurs, God makes them in the divine image. No wonder that the closing act of creation is termed "very good." What God calls into being is both good in intention and excellent in expression.

Readers in the late twentieth century may miss the radical nature of Israel's belief about creation. Among their neighbors in the Near East, whose creation documents are also known to us, Israel stood alone in proclaiming the goodness inherent in creation. Outside Israel, creation was generally believed to have been an accidental by-product of deadly rivalry between multiple deities. In those accounts, the emergence of human beings was neither helpful nor hopeful. Their lot was conflict and servile obedience to the gods, who had little interest in the good of men and women. The focus was on the heavens, not on the earth. Israel, in stark contrast, proclaimed God's intimate care and love for what was called into existence. In a world of disposable human beings, the assurance of Holy Love was, and is, welcome news. This opening theme-song is the melody that connects both Testaments and ends in the final chorus of the Revelation to St. John.

In biblical theology creation cannot be separated from history, for creation is the start-up of history. As Ludwig Köhler puts it:

> The creation of the world by God in the Old Testament is no independent fact: creation is intended to be the opening of history. The history of creation does not answer the question, "How did the world come into being?" with the answer: "God created it," but answers the question: "From where does the history of God's people derive its meaning?" with the answer: "God has given the history of His people its meaning in creation." In other words, the Creation in the Old Testament does not belong to the sphere of natural science but the history of Man.[2]

The entire primeval history, Genesis 1–11, with its wave-like progression of sin and grace, presents the growing gap between God and the world, and sounds the prelude to what God will do in response, i.e., create Israel in the Exodus. The culmination of God's frustration and outrage with humanity is the Flood. At its end, God concludes that total destruction is not the answer. The human heart will always run the risk of turning to evil, and the only useful divine response is grace:

> The LORD said in his heart, "I will never again curse the ground because of humankind, for the inclination of the human heart is evil from youth; nor will I ever again destroy every living creature as I have done." (Gen. 8:21)

That God understands our dilemma is good news.

The confusion of the nations at Babel is coupled with the call of Abraham as an indicator of how God will proceed to bring healing to the nations. From this moment, the Bible recounts the history of God's moving inexorably to redeem the world. Salvation, rather than the Fall, becomes the predominant theme. God will not deal with humankind as in the Flood, but, remembering the evil tendency of the human heart, grace is turned loose upon the human race through the descendants of Abraham and Sarah.

For Israel, the creating event was the Exodus. All that precedes it in the Bible is prelude to the supreme act of liberation and redemption at the hands of God who listens to their pain, reacts with grace and loving care, and expresses fierce anger toward those who are oppressors. The God who saved them is the same God who created them. The pattern is set for the biblical history of salvation which moves toward the final creation (or re-creation): the evil of the world will not have the last word, for destruction cannot overcome the purposes of the Maker.

How, then, shall the people of Israel relate to the One who saved them at the Sea? God's election of them demands response. That response is worked out in the Wilderness, from Sinai to the Jordan. It begins at the holy mountain, Sinai, with the giving of the Law through the person of Moses. Although Christians tend to consider that only the Ten Commandments were given there, a closer reading reveals an extensive code connected to this event, including the Holiness Code in Leviticus 17–26, which reemerges within the teachings of Jesus: "You shall be holy: for I the LORD your God am holy" (Lev. 19:2), and "you shall love your neighbor as yourself" (Lev. 19:18). The saved are called to a life in which they take on the chief attribute of the God they serve, i.e., holiness. They are to live with those around them, including the stranger or alien, as those who remember to show mercy toward others as their God has shown mercy towards them. They become the means whereby Yahweh begins the recovery and salvation of the world. Israel is set apart for the sake of the whole of creation, not just for themselves alone. This introduces a tension in which Israel is repeatedly and painfully reminded of its vocation.

The new relationship between Yahweh and Israel is one of covenant, a binding agreement, modelled on a political treaty common in the Near East, in which a lesser power enters into a bargain with a greater power in order that they (the lesser power) may receive benefits at the hands of the greater power. This "secular" form is transformed into a religious pact in which Israel consents to a pattern of life that will nurture God's saving love among them.

The covenant by which they bound themselves at Sinai was the means of turning the Hebrews into a sacred community, Israel. Yahweh entrusts Israel with the oracles of God.[3] The oracles, the word(s) of God, are embodied in a nation divinely created to bring blessing to the nations of the earth. In this sense, Israel is not just an *ethnos*, but also a *laos*—a people of God. The Sinaitic Covenant was a conditional arrangement, depending upon Israel's faithful obedience. Whenever Israel forgot they were a *laos*, disaster came crashing down on them. There was no question of Yahweh's faithfulness. His ways were certain and true. All of this was written out, and Israel became a people of the Book. The sacred Torah was the means of their salvation. To forget the Torah was to incur calamity, for God did not tolerate unholiness within the covenant nation. Thus, the sacred word was a gift of grace, for it pointed the path to *Shalom*, salvific peace.

The fact that Yahweh travelled with them in the wilderness, and that the Law could be transported as well, fitted perfectly with their belief in one God. Unlike their neighbors' deities, which were tied to locality and had to be carried about on high cultic days, Yahweh was everywhere, for the whole world was the arena of God's action.

However, the covenant of Sinai, conditional in nature, dependent upon Israel's faithfulness, was risky. Technically, it could be undone at any time, and Yahweh could abandon them. As if to answer this anxiety, there emerged in the Southern Kingdom an eternal covenant sealed with King David. In this covenant, God commits, without reservation, to an eternal covenant with the house of David. Out of this covenant comes the promise and hope for a Messiah who will be called

> Wonderful Counselor, Mighty God,
>   Everlasting Father, Prince of Peace.
> His authority shall grow continually,
>   and there shall be endless peace
> for the throne of David and his kingdom.
> He will establish and uphold it with justice
>   and with righteousness
> from this time onward and forevermore.
> The zeal of the LORD of hosts will do this. (Isaiah 9:6b-7)

This eternal covenant also demanded faithfulness, but disobedience could not terminate it. God was self-bound to keep it. For this reason, there occurred in the Old Testament numerous references to the "remnant." If even a part of the community remained faithful, the community survived and God's promise was intact. Community survival took precedence over personal survival throughout much of the Old Testament period. Only with Ezekiel does Israel begin a turn toward personal reward for faithfulness. Although this seems somewhat alien to the modern, Western mind, recall that the covenant is with the house of David, not just with David himself. As we shall see later in the New Testament section of this essay, biblical faith is never a private possession. It is always held within the context of a community of faith, in which believers commit their lives in love for God *and* neighbor. Therefore, if the community as *laos* remains, the heavenly promise is kept.

The role of *laos*, the people of God, is to bear witness to God's saving mercy. The book in which this is clearest is the little prophetic volume, Jonah. Popularly known because it is a "whale" of a story, its original purpose seems to have been to confront a growing Jewish intolerance of other nations. *Ethnos* was claiming priority over *laos*. In the story, the foreigners, from the sailors to the Ninevites, consistently behave better than Jonah, a Jew. Finally, Jonah arrives in Nineveh—the cruelest of Israel's ancient enemies—and proclaims the word of judgment from God. Utter repentance occurs in the city. God withdraws the divine word of judgment, relents, and spares the city. Such mercy is incomprehensible to the prophet. Jonah cannot understand that God's justice is tempered with grace, as was recognized in the conclusion of the Flood story. Klaus Koch declares that this book represents "the prophecy of conversion, taken to its ultimate conclusion."[4] In the post-exilic period faith began to change its expression. There was a longing for the time when God would speak directly to the people, either through prophets or epiphanies. The past, in which the nation had an intimate knowledge of God, through both deliverance and judgment, was suddenly too far away.

Although Israel fervently wished to return to a God who could be immanently apprehended, they were unsuccessful. Yahweh, the transcendent One, was beyond them. The salvation-history, passed on by the written word, offered less and less immediate help to them. They, and their forebears, had sinned too greatly. The cost of their transgression had nearly eradicated them. All that was left for them was the future. Yesterday could not be reentered. Today held little promise. But tomorrow God could, and would, fulfill the promises of old.

In this shift of focus, Israel's scriptures and traditions provided the necessary resources. The dynamic concept of the divine word was at hand. God's word, when delivered by a prophet, had a life of its own. It would continue to live until its purpose was complete. Initially, Israel probably expected the prophetic word to come to fullness in a relatively short period. However, many of the remembered "words" had remained unfulfilled. Therefore, they reckoned, God must be holding them until they find completion in a more distant moment.

Couple the understanding of divine "words" with the Exodus traditions and suddenly the future glows more brightly. The Exodus began a movement into the future, a future in which God had led the people through a painful period of want and death in the Wilderness until the Jordan was crossed. Now, every new "wilderness" experience could be interpreted in the light of the first one. A rather latent eschatology began to blossom with possibility. The God, who was currently somewhat unreachable, would return to their midst in the future. Israel became confident that this would be so. As long as they kept the words of promise in their midst, they could wait. The good news was that God had not orphaned them. They would yet be saved. Attention to the future increased. Eschatology, the belief about the last things, emerged with vigor. Fortunes would then be reversed, evil punished, the righteous healed.

Malachi, who concludes the Old Testament, views things through "eschatological" eyes, and points toward the time of Jesus and the birth of Christianity:

> See, the day is coming, burning like an oven, when all the arrogant and all evildoers will be stubble; the day that comes shall burn them up, says the LORD of hosts, so that it will leave them neither root nor branch. But for you who revere my name the sun of righteousness shall rise, with healing in its wings. You shall go out leaping like calves from the stall. And you shall tread down the wicked, for they will be ashes under the soles of your feet, on the day when I act, says the LORD of hosts.
>
> Remember the teaching of my servant Moses, the statutes and ordinances that I commanded him at Horeb for all Israel.
>
> Lo, I will send you the prophet Elijah before the great and terrible day of the LORD comes. He will turn the hearts of parents to their children and the hearts of children to their parents, so that I will not come and smite the land with a curse. (Malachi 4:1-6)

The New Testament

Jesus' biblical context for opening his mission was the Old Testament. The movement of faith, as discussed above, was not unfamiliar to either him or his intended audience. However, some four to five centuries had elapsed since the time of Malachi. During this "intertestamental period" the eschatology of Israel had become overheated. In the two centuries surrounding Jesus, more than one Jew claimed messiahship. There was a certain kind of spiritual impatience for the ancient promises to be fulfilled. Given the historical reality that the Romans ruled the land, the biblical hope of deliverance was more and more understood in nationalistic terms. The old tension between *ethnos* and *laos* was at work. Into this charged atmosphere Jesus was born.

Jesus, the incarnate one, came healing, preaching, and teaching. The summary of what he taught is found in Mark 1:15, "The time is fulfilled, the kingdom of God has come near; repent, and believe in the good news." Note what Jesus does here. First, he proclaims that the long awaited time of God, the fulfillment of ancient prophetic words, now surrounds the people. The present is the most opportune time imaginable. The immanent rule of God is so close that people can be touched by it. The Jewish faith held that the inbreaking reign of God would bring with it an incredible burst of divine power, so that things which had happened in the distant past could happen again. Evil's sway would be undone. And Jesus proclaimed that the power of God was that near. Forgiveness did not have to be earned. One had only to believe. For those whose sins were legion and who had not the time or resources to do as the Pharisees did, this gospel was miraculous, invigorating, life-renewing.

In Jesus, biblical faith holds, God begins the reclamation of creation, and none can finally defend against him. As Jesus stated in the Sermon on the Mount, "Blessed are the meek, for they will inherit the earth" (Matt. 5:5). The creation is even now being wrested from the principalities and powers. To all but those in power, this was an awesome gospel.

To open oneself to this world-transforming power, one had only to do two things: repent, and believe in the good news. Repentance was the key, for one must be divested of the evil in this world in which all share. To be sorrowful and repentant for participating in the evil forces opposed to God was essential. John the Baptist had already made this abundantly clear. But he had no other gospel. Jesus, as God's savior for the world, spelled it out in the words above and amply illustrated it by parable and healing. Nothing, no one, was beyond the saving reach of God. *Believe in the good news!* This was the offer of God, Jesus asserted, and it was the "pearl of greatest price."

One could be embraced by the power of God with the full assurance that s/he was the object of heavenly grace. In short, what Jesus did was to draw the power of future hopes—eschatology—into the present. Whatever one may hope that God will do for her/him in the future is possible now, Jesus taught. Is it any wonder that the masses responded to his teaching and found healing along the way?

Jesus' proleptic way of handling eschatology, the doctrine of last things, resulted in a certain tension of its own. Although the power of God was fully present now, the final recreation of the whole world would have to wait for a while. Where Jesus differed from contemporary thought was in the conviction that one could now enter into the Kingdom of God with all of its life-changing force. One did not have to abide until the end came. No longer was it necessary to speculate about when the Day of the Lord would come. Forgiveness, grace, and love from God allowed the change formerly associated with the end-time to occur *today*. This is the sense of Jesus' statement, "do not worry about tomorrow" (Matt. 6:34). God's power is available immediately—one of Mark's favorite words.

The Jewish right (the Sadducees), the Jewish left (the Pharisees), and the Roman Empire did not understand the nuances of Jesus' proclamation. To them, he was but another rebel and had to be stopped in order to preserve the "status quo." Together they conspired, but the Romans killed him (a reality that the Christian world is only now beginning to acknowledge, after centuries of genocide and holocaust). Crucifixion was followed by despair. Perhaps the future which Jesus had anticipated in the present was still only future.

But the resurrection changed that. With the raising of Jesus by God, the preaching and life of Jesus are confirmed from on high. Only a centurion anticipated this (proleptically?) in Matthew 27:54: "Truly this man was God's Son!" The resurrection corroborated Jesus' assurance of God's timely nearness. The wonderful power of God had truly entered the creation with a totally unprecedented creation—the dead was raised! The New Era had begun. The reign of God had come on earth as in heaven. This is the heart of biblical faith. The way to God runs through Jesus, the exalted One, the Savior and Lord of life.

Although Paul contributed mightily to the nascent church in numerous ways, nothing may have been more important than his ability to make clear to many of the earliest Christians what God had accomplished, and begun, in and through Jesus Christ. As Victor Paul Furnish puts it:

> Clearly, Paul understands the gospel to be something more than just a message about God, or Christ, or salvation. He is thinking of it first of all as *an event*—specifically, as the event of God's own powerful, saving presence and activity. It is delivered not just "in word" but "in power" (1 Thess. 1:5). It is not just a recital of ideas, but the "revealing" of God's righteousness "through faith for faith."[5]

Jesus was not just a holy person or prophet, he was, and is, the very incarnation of God. This event, as all other saving events such as the Exodus, took place in this world, in the midst of history. Unlike other saving events, Jesus was the supreme event, the hinge on which the former era swung into the new era. The atonement through Jesus Christ was for all, for all time: "at the right time Christ died for the ungodly" (Rom. 5:6), and "one man's act of righteousness leads to justification and life for all . . . so that, just as sin exercised dominion in death, so grace might also exercise dominion through justification leading to eternal life through Jesus Christ our Lord" (Rom. 5:18-21).

Just as the first creation in Genesis 1 and 2 was the beginning of God's work within history, so the event of Jesus Christ is the start of a new creation. In more than one place, but most notably in 1 Corinthians 15, the "resurrection" chapter, Paul compares the initial creation to the time of Christ:

> Thus it is written, "The first man, Adam, became a living being"; the last Adam [Jesus Christ] became a life-giving spirit. . . . The first man was from the earth, a man of dust; the second man is from heaven. (1 Cor. 15:45-47)

In Christ, who is preexistent and reigns from the time of the resurrection, God has entered the world completely, overcoming the fear that God is remote from the pain and destruction wrought by evil. Until the time of Jesus, all suffered both the sin and temporality of the first man, Adam. From the event of Christ on, all are welcomed by God into the life of the spirit wherein believers are clothed in immortality. The stronghold of evil, *death*, is overwhelmed by eternal *life*, through our Lord Jesus Christ. Because it happened within "our" history, salvation is universally intended. Jesus Christ died for all.

The universal intention of the salvation offered through Jesus

Christ is evidenced in two major contexts in the New Testament. The first of these is the Day of Pentecost. The visitation of the Holy Spirit, as of fire, undid the curse of the Tower of Babel, when nations were separated from one another by language. At Pentecost, people of "every nation under heaven" (Acts 2:5) heard the gospel in their own native tongues and believed. It has been rightly suggested that Pentecost was God's way of creating a people, a *laos*, not bound by *ethnos*, who would proclaim to all the world God's "deeds of power" (v. 11). As one layman said, "Pentecost is not about tongues, but about ears." Suddenly the whole world could hear God, whereas only the Jews would hear in the old era.

The second breakthrough came in response to Pentecost. Paul recognized that God in Christ was not meant for the Jews alone, and with this spiritual insight, the earliest churches moved beyond such ethnic practices as circumcision and proclaimed that one does not have to submit to their cultic laws in order to be "in Christ". Cultic laws and circumcision were cast aside. After some internal wrangling, the Jerusalem council confirmed Paul's missionary work among the Gentiles. This was extraordinary good news for all the world!

To accept the gospel of Jesus Christ required faith. As Leander Keck reminds us, "Faith as a personal decision and commitment was endemic to Christianity from the start, because one became a Christian by believing a message, not by being faithful to inherited religious beliefs and customs."[6] It does matter what one believes and what one does about it. Those who respond with faith in Jesus Christ, make it known to others through deeds of loving self-sacrifice and bearing witness to the Lord, as well as obedience in their moral living.

Discipleship, although it requires a personal decision, is lived out in community. However, this community is different from other human communities, because it is the very "Body of Christ," in which all are interrelated in representing Christ to the world. All are gifted by the Spirit for service to God, but no person's gifts make him/her superior to any other. Christian discipleship is marked by humility, not pride, by concern for the whole church, by care not to divide it—one of the most grievous of all sins. Faith, witness, and obedience are inseparable and essential for extending the Evangel in order for the world to be reconciled to God, its creator, its Father.

The disciple lives with an assurance that God is intimately involved in human history, saves him/her now, and will finally bring all of creation under the salvation brought near in Jesus Christ, the

Lord. Such hope, such good news cannot be kept to oneself, for the gospel is not the property of the disciple, but of the Lord. In all circumstances, the believer faithfully speaks about and points to the marvelous power of God as revealed in Jesus Christ. Just as Jesus died to save the world, so the believer is willing to suffer in order for the salvation of the world to be brought nearer to its final state, when Jesus brings the New Jerusalem on earth and all are caught up in the day of glory. The final salvation is within history, on the earth, and the creation is restored to its original pristine state.

Summary

Biblical faith is neither simplistic nor rigid, for God is neither. The revelation presented to the world through the Bible tells of a God who crafts the creation with love, makes humanity in the divine image, announces that that which is created is very good, deals with humankind primarily through grace, and so loves the world that God becomes flesh and dwells among us in the person of Jesus in order that all may be saved.

This God, the one God in three persons, began history with creation and continued to be present in the world to deliver it from sin and death. Biblical faith claims that from the beginning men and women have witnessed God's saving—and sometimes judging—activities in the world. These witnesses passed onto succeeding generations the reports, that others may believe. Theologically, this means that God will not abandon what is divinely created, regardless of how flawed it becomes. Transcendence is always tempered with immanence and vice versa. However, God in humility and service was made known to the world in Jesus Christ, who

> ... emptied himself, taking the form of a slave, being born in human likeness. And being found in human form, he humbled himself and became obedient to the point of death—even death on a cross. Therefore God also highly exalted him and gave him the name that is above every name, so that at the name of Jesus every knee should bend, in heaven and on earth and under the earth, and every tongue should confess that Jesus Christ is Lord, to the glory of God the Father. (Phil. 2:7-11)

All of this happened within time and space and is not to be viewed as a theological abstraction.

Second, biblical faith holds that believers experience the power of God in the present as those who have already passed from the power of death into the power of eternal life. Nevertheless, the church constantly draws strength from the future in which God will finally bring evil to heel and a new heaven and a new earth will emerge eternally victorious. Through the sacraments of baptism and the Lord's Supper, the faithful are graced for the present life in the Spirit.

Third, biblical faith is lived out within community. This is not surprising. Faith is expressed and passed on through the word (of Scripture) and the Word (Jesus Christ). Word—language—is communal by nature. Word is the means by which people communicate with one another, and, in our context, the means of God communicating with believers. In the Old Testament, the community was primarily Israel, and, in the New Testament, it was the church, the Body of Christ. Neither concept allowed space for persons to hold faith privately and apart form other believers. The final vision of hope is for a city—a community—where the saints will join one another in the constant worship of God and the Lamb.

Fourth, the community of faith must be ever vigilant to the marginalized of the world—the orphan, the widow, the stranger, the alien/immigrant, the "little ones," the last, the poor, the oppressed. Why is this so? In the Old Testament, the answer is to Israel, "Remember that you were a slave in the land of Egypt, and the LORD your God brought you out from there . . . " (Deut. 5:15). In the New Testament, the answer is to the church, "Once you were not a people, but now you are God's people; once you had not received mercy, but now you have received mercy" (1 Peter 2:10). When they, Israel and the church, were nobodies, God spoke up for them and acted to save them. So now the church must do the same.

What then is the work of evangelism but to tell the world the truth, God's truth, about the divine love that dwells among us through the work of the Holy Spirit. Disciples are called not so much to tell their own stories as to tell God's story as unfolded in history and culminating in Jesus Christ our Lord. To do this, persons of faith are called to lives of holiness, so that they may be holy as God is holy. Moral uprightness is joined with justice and mercy in holiness, and nurtured by devotion and deeds of service as a part of the whole church. The Body of Christ mediates God's salvation for the whole world.

As Israel was often trapped by its nationalist aspirations, so the church is tempted to see discipleship through the eyes of *ethnos*, rather than *laos*. However, the mission of the church is to the world, not just to its most comfortable "corners." Disciples, who share in the resurrection of Christ, are called to lay down their lives for those outside the church.

In conclusion, biblical faith points the church to the mission of sharing the gospel, in word and deed, with all who are yet under the power of evil that they may be saved. If God's goal is "to save the world" then disciples must avoid even the appearance of being provincial in matters of faith and mission. Rather, Christian disciples are privileged to tell joyfully the good news of the Evangel, knowing full well that God is with us—Emmanuel.

CHAPTER 2

Evangelism in a Wesleyan Perspective

R. Sheldon Duecker

MAINSTREAM PROTESTANTISM, in the forms we have known it, will not survive this century without a third Great Awakening of some sort or other!"[1] So wrote Albert Outler in 1976. At the end of the twentieth century, it looks as if Outler's prophecy may be fulfilled: "the entropy of mainline Protestantism,"[2] "dead end for the mainline,"[3] and the "collapse of mainline religion"[4] are frequently heard epitaphs for the church.

United Methodist membership has declined for three decades. This is not because people are leaving The United Methodist Church for other churches. We "gain more than we lose to other religious traditions like fundamentalists and pentecostals."[5] We decline in membership because we have not continued to recruit and receive persons on confession of faith. We have forgotten how to evangelize.

In recent decades United Methodists have relied upon confirmation classes as their primary evangelistic method. This nurturing method has not been effective. Wade Clark Roof believes that "the fastest growing religious group of the past two decades is not the Assemblies of God or the Southern Baptist Convention, but the alumni association of liberal Protestant confirmation classes."[6] Here and there we see flickers of hope in the Disciple Bible Study, the emphasis on restoring the office of Class Leader, and the Covenant Discipleship movement. There has not yet been a spread, however, of new life across the church.

Given these circumstances it is essential that we explore our Wesleyan heritage. The spiritual roots from Wesley's experiences nurtured and sustained previous generations. Perhaps we can connect with them in fresh ways and discover new sustenance that will inform, inspire and challenge us to more faithful discipleship. Our spiritual roots were grounded in a church renewal movement. The Wesleyan revival aimed to renew a contented and comfortable church. Recovery of this tradition may open us to the renewing power and presence of the Holy Spirit of God.

The Threefoldness of Grace

Grace was the theme of Wesley's preaching and writing, and grace available to all persons was the central message of the Wesleyan revival:

> All the blessings which God hath bestowed upon man, are of his ... free, undeserved favor; ... man having no claim to the least of his mercies. It is free grace indeed that 'formed man of the dust of the ground, and breathed into him a living soul,' and stamped on that soul the image of God, and 'put all things under his feet.' The same free grace continues in us, at this day, life, and breath, and all things. For there is nothing we are, or have, or do, which can deserve the least thing at God's hand. 'All our works, thou, O God! hast wrought in us.'. . . whatever righteousness may be found in man, this is . . . the gift of God.[7]

For fifty years Wesley traveled across England, Ireland, and Scotland, standing out-of-doors, or in pulpits in university chapels, or in impressive church buildings, or in small, plain chapels, preaching some 40,000 sermons which nearly always told of God's grace. His favorite phrase, "the way of salvation," was based on the fact that grace enables persons to be on such a spiritual journey.

Wesley's concept of grace was dynamically operative in three modes—prevenient, justifying, and sanctifying. This message of universal love was so powerful it motivated Wesley to go to the fields and street corners and the parks where people worked, played, and gathered. Many who saw the man and heard the message responded with wonder and joy.

Prevenient Grace

Wesley believed and clearly stated in his later preaching that no person who was outside of Christ was totally bereft of the grace of God.[8] Wesley saw God's grace as encompassing "all the 'drawings' of the Father', the desires after God, . . . all that 'light' wherewith the Son of God 'enlighteneth everyone that cometh into the world, showing every man 'to do justly, to love mercy, and to walk humbly with his God.'"⁹ "God breathes into us every good desire, and brings every good desire to good effect."¹⁰ "The very first motion of good is from above, as well as the power which conducts it to the end."¹¹

God's prevenient grace makes the response of people possible and encourages the first step into the life of Christian discipleship. This is the first word to those caught in the web of drugs. This is the first word to the young woman who is bearing a child out of wedlock and who doesn't know where to turn. This is the first word to be spoken to the couples whose marriages are crumbling. This is the first word we have to give to the twenty-somethings who have serious questions about the purpose of their life. Are United Methodists in those places speaking the word of God's prevenient grace? All too often we sit in our comfortable offices and leave it to others.

How many people with a thirst for God's love are standing on corners in cities, bustling through malls, sitting in front of television sets waiting for a person to meet with them, to say and be the word of grace in today's world? Who is to tell them, if they don't happen into one of our churches, that prevenient grace, God's universal grace "free for all and free in all" energizes and awakens? "The whole world, by prevenient grace, hears the call to come home to the family of God. Whether or not they are Christian, they yearn for the bread of life; they are hungry for spiritual food."¹²

In his November, 1994, report on the work in Russia, Bishop Ruediger Minor said that "the God of grace revealed in Jesus Christ has been there all those years of atheistic communism sustaining its people amidst suffering, terror, persecution and oppression." God's prevenient grace in Christ is working in an anticipatory way in the lives of all people wherever they may be. Belief in the prevenient grace is the affirmation that Christ goes before us, is already *there* and will meet us *there*. Our evangelistic task "is . . . stirring up the human spirit, . . . awakening faith—inviting and persuading [people] to attend the word within."¹³

People in England could thank the Church of England for forcing Wesley into the streets. Are we in The United Methodist Church forcing evangelisticly minded ministers into other denominations? Are we responsible for moving people from our churches to other denominations? Do we know that people come to church week after week "because God's prevenient grace gives them the instinct to know that this is where they can find the very substance of living bread. . . . The irony is that we are so busy grinding out our churchly business, that we fail to see their ravenous consumption of the occasional crumbs of spiritual food they happen to find...."[14]

Justifying Grace

Justifying grace "is the forgiveness of all our sins."[15] To be justified is to live with a "moment by moment sense of pardon, experienced by faith."[16] The only condition for justification is that a person have faith in the merits of Christ's atoning work. This faith is itself a gift of God.

Would not the millions of alcoholics be stunned with this news? As they look to the bottle for relief from the pressures of today, can we not find a way to demonstrate that "moment by moment" God is able to help? Who will preach this message to an alcoholic? If we are unable to tell them this part of the message we will be unable to show them that the effects of justification are, "the peace of God, a 'peace that passeth all understanding,' and a 'rejoicing in hope in the glory of God,' 'with joy unspeakable and full of glory.'"[17] Justification from the Wesleyan perspective is a dynamic reality. Time and again the believer, under the wooing of God's Holy Spirit, comes back to this doorway of the Christian life.

Our preaching should not be calculated to induce guilt. Everyone has enough of that. Our preaching should focus on God's grace that can be replenished. "Christ loved me and gave himself for me."[18] How sweet that sound! But who will preach it? And to whom? The Jims, Janes, Abduls, Minervas, and Sarahs of our world need to hear that their sin is forgiven and that they can have a rebirth of their spirit. At the same time, they must not be permitted to hear "words of grace without words of judgment."[19] Our preaching must require participation in salvation, spiritual discipline as a prerequisite for sanctification, and faith in Christ as the only prerequisite for receiving God's grace. A fundamental problem is that we preach grace "to a society that is under the illusion that they deserve everything they can get and have gotten."[20]

Wesley warned his preachers, as we must warn ours, that self-satisfied moral people do not like to be told that they are sinners. He warned his preachers that their preaching would "alienate hearts from you and open mouths against you." But there were and are many John and Jane Does who suffer in silence waiting for the words of liberating grace. Wesley said "there can be no true peace, no solid joy, either in time or eternity," without justification.[21] Albert Outler restated this, "By faith—and faith alone!—uptight lives are relaxed, trapped lives liberated, arrogant lives humbled, soiled lives cleansed, slouching lives raised up to tiptoe, empty lives filled, life unto death turned into life unto life."[22]

Sanctifying Grace

Justification is the beginning, the doorway to sanctification which begins to open at the moment of grace-engendered faith. Wesley compared the entry into the Christian life with natural birth. Justification is the threshold of sanctification: "As in the natural birth a [person] is born at once and then grows larger and stronger by degrees, so in the spiritual birth a [person] is born at once, and then gradually increases in spiritual stature and strength."[23] Everyone hearing the gospel must understand that acceptance of God's love is a radically life-changing process. It is a warming of the heart, a quickening of purpose, a desire to aid others, to seek for the mind that was in Christ Jesus. Yet this is only the beginning. We must tell the searchers that they need to proceed in their spiritual development like a child, to grow into maturity in love.

Sanctification is a thorough inward change by the grace of God in our hearts. It is growth toward Christian perfection which Wesley perceived as "loving God with all our heart, mind, soul and strength" so that "all thoughts, words, and actions are governed by pure love."[24] Sanctification changes the human will. It demands an intentionality that, through the gift of grace, a person accept the will of God. Obedience to God's will is to become so habitual that the will loses its tendency to resist God's sovereign grace.

People may find this a startling new message. The grace of Christ initiates and in that grace we actively respond "working out our own salvation in the power of the Holy Spirit." Salvation is neither "going to heaven" nor "going to paradise" nor even "a blessing which lies on the other side of death."[25] The wholeness of life which Christ's grace creates is evidenced in holiness of love for God and neighbor. Perfecting this love leads to the development of disciplines for works of piety and works of mercy. The discipline of works of piety and works of mercy is what "keeps us with Christ" as we move toward that perfect love transcending all other loves.

In sanctification there is transformation of the inner life as we are restored to the image of God. But God's love transforms the daily lives of those who respond to it. Grace requires response. In addition, holiness, or the results of grace, must be demonstrated daily in loving devotion to God and loving acts for neighbor. The goal is an outward holiness that springs from an inward holiness of heart. Here is the dialectic so difficult to grasp and maintain. Grace is *Christ's* doing, but grace empowers *our* doing. The Wesleyan message is, "Responsibility in grace, and grace in responsibility."

Faith, a personal response to God, is the only condition for sanctification. However, to grow in grace and to remain in grace entails repentance. Wesley called this "evangelical repentance," and held it to be subsequent to justification. After such repentance sin may no longer reign supreme but there remains "proneness to evil," "the carnal mind," "a heart bent to backsliding," a tendency to self-will, and other evidences of sin within.[26] Sin is ever present. The Christian life, for Wesley, was an optimistic one given the working of grace. It is nevertheless a vigilant one given the constant lurking of sin.

Wesley was "relentless in emphasizing the essential character of the concrete demonstration of divine love dwelling in our hearts. Love was far more than an attitude for Wesley. It was a pattern of action."[27] This action took various forms, such as a constant presence with the poor, personal charity, and the organization of clinics, cooperatives and credit unions. Wesley's gospel changed individuals, the church, and society. It was not captive to the fads of the moment. In the final years of the twentieth century the millions of Jane and John Does who run corporations, raise children, and struggle to make a living need to hear about the grace that is free yet rigorous. Only a grace that justifies can sanctify. We cannot leave the concern to "work out one's salvation" to chance or individual initiative. Such is not Wesleyan evangelism. Wesley insists on getting the order straight. God will heal our brokenness and restore our wholeness but not without our exercise of responsive grace. A "prudential means of grace" must be operative to provide effective support and accountability.

The Structure of the Revival

Proclamation

John Wesley was firmly grounded in the tradition of the Anglican Church. When Methodism was portrayed as pretending to be "a new discovery in religion" Wesley responded, "We pretend no such thing.

We aver, it is the one, old religion: as old as the Reformation, as old as Christianity, as old as Moses, as old as Adam."[28] Wesley believed he was preaching the fundamental doctrine of the church. The two constant themes in his message after 1738 were "salvation by faith alone," and the "witness of the Spirit." These were both the result of Wesley's own search for and discovery of the power of the Holy Spirit in his life."[29]

Wesley's intention was to preach "plain truth for plain people." Thousands stood in the open air to hear, feel, and learn the message he preached. The Anglican Church and the nonconformist churches[30] had a disdainful attitude toward the common people, but Wesley had a passion to preach the gospel to all persons and to bring all persons to salvation. If that were the attitude of United Methodism today, it, like Wesley in his day, would stand in sharp contrast to prevailing views.

Wesley's view of God's purpose for him and the Methodist people was "to reform the nation, more particularly the church; to spread scriptural holiness over the land."[31] Wesley's "reputation as a preacher has probably been overestimated,"[32] but people responded to his message of free grace for all. God's grace made no distinction between persons. Marginalized and dehumanized people heard the message eagerly. This universal grace "compelled Wesley . . . to the open fields, to the marketplaces, the prisons, the mine shafts, and the bedsides of those dying in poverty in the squalor of a tenement flat."[33] His confidence grew as people responded to his preaching. His hesitancy was "swept aside by the remarkable response to his preaching."[34]

Wesley's field preaching was the most effective method he employed. This was the initial point of contact for most of those who came into the Methodist societies. A total of 25,000 people heard him during the first two weeks of April, 1739, when he began field preaching, with the crowds ranging from 1,000 to 6,000 on those eight occasions. Wesley's form of evangelism was as new and alien to him as it is to us. He liked the surety of the church, the sanctity of the sacraments, the colors of the robes and stoles. He was uncertain in the open field, but people came to hear the gospel. They came because he proclaimed a message for the common person. How novel is this idea? Jesus did the same thing. Both Wesley and Jesus were heard because they went where the people were.

Wesley is both a model for and a challenge to many of our churches who consider their ministry as primarily chaplaincy—caring for the members of the church. Even those who live within sight of the church building are ignored. Revitalization efforts to change this perception bring mixed results primarily because there is a lack of commitment to the message, and our clergy are ill equipped to preach the good news to the common person.

Societies

Wesley maintained a deep respect for, and loyalty to, the Church of England. He would not support those who wanted the Methodist movement to secede from the Church of England. Wesley "knew that evangelism outside of a context of the sacramental means of grace is as finally invalid for the converted as are the means of grace for the unconverted."[35] Evangelism was to the members of the church as well as to those outside the church. Structures were formed to assist the mission to which John Wesley believed God had called the Methodists. In particular two influences helped shape the structure: the religious societies of the Church of England and the communal piety of the Moravians.

Within the Church of England religious societies had been operating more than thirty years before Wesley was born. These societies gained the full approval of the church authorities and were to "keep close" to the Church of England. Only confirmed members of the Church of England were permitted to participate in these societies. They attracted persons who wanted to develop a more disciplined spiritual life and satisfy the spiritual hunger not being met by the established church. No doctrinal standards were required for membership. The focus was on the pattern of their discipleship. Their piety increasingly led them to the practical works of caring for the poor, relieving debt, visiting the sick, providing for orphans, and setting up about a hundred schools in London and the suburbs.[36]

The Moravian influence on Wesley led him to add the element of spiritual nurture to the societies. "The religious societies supplied only the body to Methodism, the Moravians gave it a soul; under their influence the empty vessels were again filled, but the wine was different."[37] The societies were organized in response to spiritual needs. Persons who wished to be guided in Christian understanding and living came to Charles and John Wesley for help and fellowship. There were too many to talk with them one by one as often as they needed it. So John Wesley extended an invitation, "If you will all of you come together every Thursday, in the evening, I will gladly spend some time with you in prayer, and give you the best advice I can."[38] "Thus arose, without any previous design on either side, what was afterwards called a society."[39]

Societies were formed because Wesley was concerned for persons and their growth into holiness. They effectively conserved the fruits of the revival. This, however, was a serendipitous result and not the reason for forming them. Wesley described a society as

> a company of men having the form, and seeking the power of godliness, united in order to pray together, to receive the word of exhortation, and to watch over one another in love, that they may help each other to work out their salvation.[40]

There was only one condition for membership in a society. It was the desire on the part of persons "to flee from the wrath to come, and to be saved from their sins."[41] There were no doctrinal requirements for membership but the members were committed to practice specific behavior. The meetings of the society were occasions when the members of the various classes in each society came together for worship or fellowship. There was to be no doctrinal disputation in the meetings. Doctrinal standards were set by Wesley and the preachers in the annual Conference.

Wesley visited the societies for purposes of instruction, reproof, and discipline. In 1759 he visited a society at Hempnail: "I met the society at seven and told them in plain terms that they were the most ignorant, self-conceited, disjointed society that I knew in the three kingdoms. And God applied it to their hearts so that many were profited, but I do not find that one was offended."[42] How many times have we been so blunt to a cabinet or to a church? Wesley knew how to "speak the truth in love." In this practice lies a lesson for us today.

At times Wesley was disappointed with what he found. On one occasion he met a society at five in the afternoon to explain the nature and use of meeting in a class, "Upon inquiry I found, we have now about five hundred members. But an hundred and fifty of these do not pretend to meet at all. Of these therefore I make no account. They hang but on a single thread."[43] We have a process for removing people from our churches with little more than *pro forma* attempts to contact them. The disappointment at the losses of souls hardly crosses our minds. Too often we rejoice if reduced membership lowers our apportionments.

Classes and Bands

The societies, as originally formed, were structures within the Anglican Church. They were held together, and made vital, by the classes and bands. Wesley's understanding of Christian discipleship made two distinctions. First, there was the family of God throughout the world reached by prevenient grace. These needed to be taught, healed, fed, and loved. Second, there were those who were in the community called the church. In that setting the gospel was proclaimed to provide teaching, healing, feeding, and loving. These were called to disciplined Christian discipleship to be leaven for both the church and the world. It is clear from Methodist history that while God's salvation is for all the world not everyone is going to become a Christian disciple. On the other hand, some will be called into deeper discipleship to provide power and strength for the entire church.

Classes and bands were the groups that provided a means of implementing accountable discipleship among society members. The classes and bands were reflective and accountability groups where people learned a new way of life. It was a way of life which would govern their relationships with God and with other persons. It was a way of life which would influence the getting and spending of wealth. It was a way of life which provided stable fellowship and deep friendships. Classes and bands were organized to help "work out salvation." Their existence and effectiveness went a long way toward explaining the difference between the Methodist movement and other revivals during the same period which flourished and then faded away.

Classes and bands were little churches within the larger church of the society (*ecclesiolae in ecclesia*). They grew out of the need to move from the masses to a setting for more personal instruction and more intimate relationships. They recognized that discipleship is not a solitary activity. Christian living requires spiritual direction. This, the class leader and the group provided. Classes were for those who were seeking salvation; bands were for those who had found it. Class meetings were "a major factor in bringing persons to a point of Christian commitment as well as confirming them in it afterwards."[44] Bands were restricted to those who were already justified and wanted and needed "some means of closer union."[45] Classes were a "port of entry" into Christian discipleship and bands were for those who were already on the journey.

Meeting in a class was a condition for continued membership in the society; meeting in a band was not. "Class tickets" were issued by the class leaders and served to admit a member into the meeting of the society. A "band ticket" permitted attendance also and represented a higher level of spiritual attainment. Three consecutive absences were considered self expulsion. This was not a formal rule but it was a common practice.

Bands followed the Moravian plan of division by age, gender and marital status. Classes were formed according to where people lived. In small societies there might have been only one class. In larger societies there were more than one and these might include some segregated by gender while others were mixed. Classes were usually larger than the five to ten members to which bands were limited. Bands were more intimate gatherings and permitted more probing discussions. Bands were introduced several years before classes. Since he had already proved the worth of this Moravian institution in Georgia and in London it was a natural step to use it in the societies.

The class began in Bristol in 1742 as a financial expedient, and the giving of money remained one element of the covenant. "Class money," usually a penny a week plus a shilling a quarter was given, noted in the record and devoted to the needs of the poor and the propagation of the gospel. The effectiveness of the structure was not lost on Wesley, and soon he had expanded its responsibility to include spiritual accountability.

Bands elected their own leaders from among the members; class leaders were appointed by Wesley or one of his assistants. Class leaders were always laypersons. The duties of the class leader were specified in the General Rules. They met weekly with the preacher to report on the spiritual welfare of the members and brought the money which they had collected. Class leaders were central to the revival. They became as skilled a group of spiritual mentors as the church has ever produced. As these persons grew in their own discipleship many of them became preachers in the movement.

Accountability was an important element for both bands and classes. Bands were subject to more rigorous oversight than the classes. The rules of the bands called for a searching examination of each member by the other members. These examinations were very personal and probing regarding temptations or known sins committed since the last meeting. The members of each group were bound together in a covenant which formed the basis for accountability. Early Methodists found that they needed something to sustain them in their journey. They came to see that an active, personal relationship with God, obedience to a shared covenant, and the class meetings were essential factors in their discipleship.

Classes were bound by the General Rules and bands by the Rules of the Bands. These rules were developed by John Wesley and the preachers and reviewed and revised annually in the annual Conference if that was necessary.[46] Band members were expected to "abstain from evil carefully, to maintain good works zealously, and to attend on all the ordinances of the church constantly."[47] In time the class meeting became the basic structure. Where the class leader became skilled and spiritually perceptive the distinction between the two groups became imprecise. However, even then, the bands were not entirely neglected.[48]

Training leaders today to be for United Methodism what the class and band were to Wesley's day should be a priority. The efforts of David Lowes Watson and others to develop Covenant Discipleship Groups is one attempt to recover some of the dynamic of this structure in a contemporary fashion. The small group emphases of classes and bands were quite intense as members counseled and critiqued each other. People today are familiar with this small group process but have had little experience in using it for spiritual development. It would be a small step in many congregations to institute a rigorous program of spiritual nurture using their existing small groups.

The Dialectic of Justification and Sanctification: A Clue to Wesleyan Evangelization

Wesley identifies the dialectic in his sermon on "Justification by Faith." Justification implies "what God *does for us* through his Son; the other (sanctification) what he *works in us* by his Spirit."[49] Both are distinct acts of God and yet are inseparable. One (justification) takes away the *guilt* of sin; the other (sanctification) takes away the *power* of sin. The first is an *instantaneous act* of God depending on the condition of a believer's faith. The second is a *lifelong process* in which the believer moves toward perfection in love.

One does not move sequentially from justification to sanctification: "at the same time that we are justified, . . . *sanctification* begins.

In that instant we are 'born again'; 'born from above'; 'born of the Spirit.'"[50] The tension between God's vision of holiness (perfect love) and human performance may require us to enter the doorway of justification time and again. Christian discipleship requires a synthesis of justification and sanctification. One ignores either of them at one's peril.

One characteristic of our times is a focus on justification without moving toward sanctification. A common feeling seems to be that since I can be saved or am saved, I can do anything I so desire. "I want it, therefore I need it, therefore I deserve it." Anything goes if I want it or need it. One's own way is claimed as a "right" and obedience to God's perfecting will isn't given a second thought. On the other hand, to focus only on works leads to compulsive self-justification.[51] Secular forms of legalism abound in struggles to measure up to expectations, desperation about fitting in to the group and a morbid fear of failure. Moderns go to all kinds of extremes to prove their worth to themselves and to others.

A synthesis of these two dynamics of grace is required to move toward discipleship and holiness. Human experience led early Methodists into classes and bands for purposes of accountable discipleship. In those settings the dialectic between justification and sanctification was taken seriously as members guided, taught, chided, and supported one another into obedience which led to salvation—"love of God and love of neighbor."

Our age is yearning for this message which brings balance and direction into the spiritual life. "Millions of Americans are embarking on a search for the sacred in their lives.... Some are returning to the religions of their childhoods, finding new meaning in old rituals. Others look for wisdom outside their own cultures, mixing different traditions in an individualistic stew."[52] People are left high and dry "after having squeezed out substitutes for God in sex, success and career ladders. They sense that existence is more than the sum of bodily functions and malfunctions."[53] Baby boomers are leading others in this search as they have a deep sense of their need for spirituality but are at a loss to know where to look. It is time for us to get out to where people live. We must hear their needs and respond to their search for meaning with the message of God's universal love. We must demonstrate to them what it is to grow into perfect love and challenge them to go with us on that journey.

These are our spiritual roots; they can nourish us. The class and the band are structures to help us be disciplined and nurtured as we move into perfect love. Going to where people are and speaking in plain language is the form for evangelism in the Wesleyan tradition. In our day this may mean preaching in some unorthodox places but it will also mean using television with a direct message of love and forgiveness.

We will not do it for the sake of The United Methodist Church. It is for the sake of the world that we are called to proclaim this message. God grant that we will recover the vision and have the will to go to the people and to nurture accountable disciples. The world hungers for "plain truth for plain people." The world hungers, even if it knows not, for the grace that sets us free (justifying grace) for accountable discipleship (sanctifying grace). Faithfulness to this vision could bring a new day for United Methodism.

CHAPTER 3

Evangelism in the Otterbein-Albright Tradition

George W. Bashore

ALTHOUGH MY OWN personal history is rooted deeply in the Evangelical United Brethren heritage, I make no claims that I am an adequate historian of that tradition; however, embedded in that history, my personal spiritual journey, as our United Methodist contemporary evangelistic quest, is the experiential assurance of and witness to the saving power of Jesus Christ. The early founders of both The Evangelical Church and The United Brethren in Christ Church had similar experiences to the "heart-warming" happening of John Wesley, founder of The Methodist Church. Those life-changing episodes led to a greater fervor in evangelism and to a deeper expression of communal piety.

Brief biographical sketches of four key figures from those early beginnings of these two churches will best serve to tell the story of their remarkable personal experiences of God's reality in their lives. We will note that these four—Philip William Otterbein, Martin Boehm, Jacob Albright, and John Seybert—come from different backgrounds in vocation, educational training, and faith traditions. Yet there is a commonality in assurance of faith and passion for the souls of others. Let us hear the story of theological influences in their lives and their adventures in faith.

All of these persons came under the influence of pietism. Philip William Otterbein, the co-founder of The United Brethren Church, was no stranger to the influence of piety prior to his answer to the call to go to America. His father was a pastor and teacher of the Reformed Church in Germany. William was educated at Herborn University where he and his brother, Georg, were instilled with an evangelical pietism. He was influenced by the Heidelberg Catechism which he used in his churches throughout his ministry. In his home the Heidelberg Catechism was taught, and Herborn University was founded in 1854 by Olevianus, co-author of the Heidelberg Catechism.

At Herborn, Otterbein came under the influence of John Henry Schramm and others who were advocates for *in der Tat* Christianity. Faith's strongest expression was in the deed, not in the creed. Pietism talked about the identification of conversion with regeneration, a new birth incarnated in all of life's experiences. Conversion meant a change from the externals of religion to an inner religious experience of Christ and the assurance of salvation. The inner experience of the assurance of God's salvation in Christ was to move persons from an intellectualism to a "warm heart" relationship with God which in turn influences one's behavior and passion for souls.

We have very few extant resources written by William Otterbein; however, Georg Otterbein gives us insights into the influences of the Heidelberg Catechism. He was concerned that believers should approach Scripture and catechism with personal questions derived from real life situations:

> Dialectical thinking is appropriate in theology only when it is used to answer questions raised by a person about his [her] spiritual condition . . . not a proclamation of objective faith to which the believer gives rational assent, as it was for the scholastic catechist; rather it provides the basis for one to admonish readers to pay attention to the condition of their own hearts.[1]

Conversion is more than baptism or assent to a creed for the Otterbeins. Rather it involves the entire order as outlined in the Heidelberg Catechism. New birth is the beginning of a process of becoming. Conversion is participation in the entire process outlined in the threefold steps in the Heidelberg Catechism.

The first question of the catechism is "What is your only comfort, in life and in death?" Then the second question and answer outline the order for one's pilgrimage of obedience to God. The question is "How many things must you know that you may live and die in the blessedness of this comfort?" The answer indicates, "Three. First, the greatness of my sin and wretchedness. Second, how I am freed from all my sins and their wretched consequences. Third, what gratitude

I owe to God for such redemption." The three parts of the catechism are then explicated in more detail.²

J. Steven O'Malley writes that the basis for question one "has been shifted from the classic Calvinistic theology of mystical union and election to one which places primary emphasis upon personal decision, efforts and *in der Tat* Christianity."³ The only comfort in life and death is to belong to Christ, and to be converted is to participate in these three steps of the order of salvation (*Heilsordnung*) and to climb the ladder of salvation (*Himmelsleiter*), the ladder to heaven, with the help of God's grace. Georg warned that an "endless eternity depends on these" steps. "Personal temporal decisions in this world are more important than eternal decrees in determining one's final outcome in the world to come." The influence of pietism caused the Otterbeins to remain convinced that "the only virtue worthy of the name was that which took seriously the inability of unredeemed [humanity] to act morally."⁴

In William Otterbein's only extant sermon he speaks about the wretchedness of our human condition and the necessity to recognize this state of our being without grace:

> Man's understanding is full of darkness; the will is full of wickedness and evil imaginings against God. This shows itself inwardly in a turning away of the heart from God, and outwardly in numerous works of the flesh.... From this also arise by necessity such things as fear, restlessness, shock, and confusion of conscience. And if grace does not intervene against this corruption, there must further follow eternal death, eternal corruption of soul and body.⁵

It was during Otterbein's pastorate in Lancaster, Pennsylvania, that he felt his heart "strangely warmed." Otterbein's discovery of the assurance of his salvation is a well-beloved story for former United Brethren. "Not long after he came to Lancaster, and immediately after he had preached one of his most searching discourses, a member of his congregation came to him in tears, bitterly lamenting his sins, and asked advice. Looking upon him sadly, yet tenderly, he only said: 'My friend, advice is scarce with me today.' The seeker went on his way, and Mr. Otterbein repaired to his closet, and there wrestled, like Jacob, until he obtained the forgiveness of sins, the witness of the Holy Spirit of adoption, and was filled with joy unspeakable and full of glory!"⁶

The crisis became a time of discovery of God's mystery of grace for him. Indeed a consequence was an urgency to proclaim the necessity of a personal experience of this assurance of salvation in Christ. Such an inner experience was not only an act of illumination, but it was also a steppingstone for living a life of holiness. "Christ's work is merely the 'groundwork' for our salvation, notes Otterbein, and the external hearing of the Word, participation in the sacraments, and formal adherence to the discipline of the church are all depreciated if they are not accompanied by an earnest quest for complete righteousness of life. The reign of the exalted Christ, as portrayed in the Catechism, has become the imminent reality of the 'Kingdom within' or of 'Christ in us.'"[7]

Martin Boehm, co-founder with Otterbein of The Church of The United Brethren in Christ, was raised as a Mennonite. At the age of thirty-one he was chosen by lot to be a Mennonite minister. He believed that his choice by lot was indeed a divine appointment; however, he was filled with fears and a sense of inadequacy. On the very next Sunday he was asked to preach. Although he had prepared with memorized scriptures, he could only stammer and sat down in shame. The same thing happened to him week after week. In a famous sermon preached at Isaac Long's barn in Lancaster Martin Boehm told of his experience of shame and newly discovered assurance in God's salvation.

> I had faith in prayer and prayed more fervently. While thus engaged in prayer earnestly for aid to preach, the thought rose up in my mind, or as though one spoke to me saying, "You pray for grace to teach others the way of salvation, and you have not prayed for your own salvation!" . . . while praying for myself, my mind became alarmed. I felt I was myself a poor sinner. I was lost. My agony became great. I was ploughing in the field, and kneeled down at each end of the furrow, to pray. The word, "lost," went every round with me. Midway in the field I could go no further, but sank down behind the plough, crying, "Lord, save! I am lost." And again the voice said, "I am come to seek and to save that which was lost." In a moment a stream of joy was poured over me. I praised the Lord, and left the field, and told my companion what joy I felt.
>
> As before this I wished the Sabbath far off, now I wished it were tomorrow! Sunday came. . . . I rose to tell of my experience. . . . When speaking of my lost estate, and agony of mind, some began to weep. . . . This gave me encouragement to speak of our fall and lost condition, and of repentance. . . .

... Christ will never find us, till we know that we are lost. My wife was (I am happy to be able to say to you) the next lost sinner that felt the same joy, the same love.[8]

In that congregation of one thousand assembled in Isaac Long's barn was William Otterbein. Unable to contain his own emotion, he rose, came forward and grasped Martin's hand, exclaiming "*Wir sind Brueder*" (We are brothers). This was the beginning of this team, which sparked the fire of United Brethren evangelism in this country.

One of the persons who heard the preaching of Otterbein and others with pietist influence was Jacob Albright, a farmer and tilemaker, who was to become the founder of The Evangelical Church. For years a sense of peace had eluded him. Several of his children died in 1790 from an epidemic of dysentery. He interpreted this tragedy as punishment from God. There was a growing, gnawing unrest within him, so in the midst of great despair he went to a neighbor's house for prayer and counsel. This was Adam Riegel, who was influenced by Otterbein and the United Brethren. Riegel spent many hours in prayer with Albright. Albright wrote of his experience:

> I heard the voice of consolation in my soul. I ... was convinced that since God does not desire the destruction of a sinner, but that he should turn from his way and live, he would look upon my sincere repentance ... with gracious eyes and that the merit of my Lord and his bitter suffering and death would complete the work.... Gradually every anguish of heart was removed and comfort and the blessed peace of God pervaded my soul. God's spirit bore witness with my spirit, that I was a child of God; one joyful experience followed another, and such a heavenly joy pervaded my whole being, as no pen can describe and no mortal can express.... My prayers were no longer mere entreaties but praise and hearty thanksgiving were also brought as an offering, mingled with tears of joy, to the giver of every good gift.[9]

Albright could then not contain the good news. He preached, even when his life was in danger. He was beaten severely by those who objected to a freer expression of religious faith. When he preached, those listening would have such a tremendous sense of their sin that they would plead for forgiveness from God. He emphasized repentance, faith within one's own heart, regeneration, and sanctification. He was untiring in his preaching to neighbors and German-speaking peoples, predominantly in the rural areas. His travels extended to Maryland and Virginia. He spoke with great urgency about God's judgment against sin and shared the way of salvation. He, like Otterbein, also preached a holiness of life, which included a condemnation of gambling, drunkenness, and other ungodly activities. Others hearing him began to feel an affinity to the call for personal experience and became Albright's followers. His influence was so great that one of Albright's early converts, John Walter, preached the funeral message on the text from Daniel 12:3: "Those who are wise shall shine like the brightness of the sky, and those who lead many to righteousness, like the stars forever and ever."

Another follower of Albright was John Seybert, a maker and repairer of barrels, who became a class leader, evangelist, circuit rider and bishop. He gave his life to Christ under the influence of circuit riders. We could mention many circuit riders among the early Albright people and Otterbein people. Christian Newcomer was a circuit rider matched by very few in beginnings of The United Brethren Church; however, I have chosen to mention John Seybert as a representative circuit rider for both churches. The following comments accurately characterize his ministry.

> Mile after mile he walked or rode horseback, visiting from house to house, holding meetings in homes.... He always inquired into the personal, spiritual state of the family or individual members and ... never failed to speak kindly to every child.
> He was a man taught by God, a man mighty in prayer, deeply versed in the Scriptures, for they were the fountain from which to draw his material for the remarkable sermons he delivered.... He walked with God, and held almost constant communion with Him.... In 1834 over an eleven month period he held seven "Big Meetings" (all-day evangelistic efforts often lasting into the night, and of 2 to 3 day duration), five campmeetings, traveled 4,406 miles on horseback, visited many families to pray with them, preached 300 times.... None did more in molding the expansion and character of The Evangelical Church in the midwest than John Seybert.... He traveled steadily to places "farthest out."... In 1842 he brought over the mountains of Pennsylvania to the Ohio conference 23,725 volumes.... In his round of duties no place was too far, no hour too late, no effort too great for him to counsel with a person or to preach to a gathering or to a congregation, in the interest of reaching souls for Christ's kingdom.[10]

A memorial in the Seybert United Methodist Church in Bellevue, Ohio states: *Bischof Seybert—Ein Mann nach dem Herzen Gottes. Das*

Wort Gottes war ihm eine rechte Speise fuer seine Seele ("Bishop Seybert—a man in conformity to the heart of God. The Word of God was for him the right food for his soul").

Seybert's final entry in his journal on December 28, 1859, was "One soul saved!" The *Dictionary of American Biography* says of John Seybert, "he was a man with one basic idea and his heart beat with the throb of the angels rejoicing when he could write, 'Another man has found the Savior, one soul saved.'"[11] That characterizes the assurance within these early founders of both churches, and it constitutes the urgency of proclaiming the gospel to all persons.

Although the Heidelberg Catechism never became an official standard for these churches, its influence upon Otterbein was to impact much of what took place in those early years of evangelistic outreach. The Heidelberg Catechism moves persons to meditate not only on the contemplation of the mind but also on the understanding of the heart in its real experience of the presence of Christ within, bringing about assurance of salvation and empowerment of holy living.

> It [Heidelberg] was not a mere cold theological treatise, but one of warm living faith.... The Catechism presented religion as a personal comfort and faith as a hearty confidence and assurance. Many of the questions are in the second person singular, making them direct and personal questions for the catechumens. The answers then are often in the first person, so the individuals will be responding as expressions of personal faith. This is not mere intellectualism, isolated from real life, but rather these are expressions of faith for life's experiences.[12]

Many persons in the pioneer communities longed for warm fellowship, assurance of salvation, vital preaching, and a discipline for their spiritual journeys. Communal piety was developed, as believers gathered in homes for instruction, prayer, Bible study, lively singing, and sharing of witness. Otterbein was the first in the Reformed Church to begin pietist conventicles, and he continued them throughout his ministry. The class meetings of the Methodists were models for the followers of Otterbein and Albright.

I wish to paraphrase Paul Eller in his excellent statement about Otterbein, Albright, and Martin Boehm. These were three men who were so very dissimilar in background, culture, education, social status, and churchmanship. In training, theology, and philosophy, Otterbein is widely separated from Boehm and Albright. Methodist

Bishop Francis Asbury commented that Otterbein had one of the most astute minds in America at that time. Yet for all the decisive points of difference there was a fundamental, common ground on which they stood. They were in agreement on the sorry plight of a lost world and lost humanity. They also agreed that only a divine act, God's Son, freely and knowingly accepted could assuage the spiritual sickness of humanity.

> Each called persons from infidelity, half-faith, or faith in the wrong things to a vibrant, robust personal trust in the Savior. Each called persons from the current indiscrimination between right and wrong. Each called persons from the contemporary ruthlessness, coarseness and lawlessness. Each in his own way pointed to the insufficiency of traditionalism, sacramentalism or custom to bring persons into significant relationship with God. . . . They sought to make disciples of Christ. . . . For these preachers, salvation was the first and foremost of the articles of faith.
>
> Salvation, they held, was imperative because all persons are sinners and possible because of God's mercy and His will-to-love. . . . With simple audacity, these preachers looked the proud, self-made individualist of the frontier in the eyes and declared him to be a sinner. Salvation, they held, was possible because God created man with the capacity to receive His Word, and His Son voluntarily took the sin of all upon Himself. . . . Through the work of Jesus Christ each person had been given to God but it remained for everyone to confirm what God's Son had effected. Our impotence is dissolved when Calvary is accepted and appropriated.
>
> Salvation . . . was personal. Everyone is equipped with the freedom to say "yes" or "no" to God. As anyone says "yes" that person experiences the divine gift of salvation. The core of religion is held to be God-in-the-heart, cleansing, confirming, empowering to which the religious consciousness gives decisive testimony.[13]

There was the call to repentance, faith, and holy living. Repentance was necessary, for persons were in an unredeemed condition. Several years ago during my undergraduate years at Princeton University a forum of university professors from the disciplines of philosophy, psychology, natural science, and religion were given the assignment, "Is there some common agreement in life's experiences about the nature of humankind?" After a long debate they finally came to the one common conclusion, that humankind does not live up to the fullest potential for which persons have been created. The early evangelists were convinced that such a state was an unredeemed condition in need of acceptance of God's grace in Christ alone. Repent, accept God's grace in Christ by faith and live in Christ were the themes for "spreading Scriptural holiness throughout the land." "Its (United Brethren) sermons were clear, profound and forceful, accompanied with evangelical power."[14]

Otterbein was so concerned that persons live holy lives of faith, that he required participation in a preparatory service for Holy Communion. Prior to celebrating the Eucharist a person needed to have an assurance of salvation. This assurance of salvation was both justification by faith and sanctification for the early evangelists in the Otterbein-Albright tradition.

These evangelists were so convinced of the reality of God's salvation for themselves and the desperate state of humanity, that their own souls could not rest, until they confronted others with the fallen nature of their souls and the redeeming possibility in Jesus Christ. Therefore, they had an evangelistic passion for the unreached and a missionary fervor. Wherever they found persons—in homes, barns, fields, taverns, and other gathering places—they witnessed to their own discovery of Christ's redeeming power. They were deeply versed in Scripture; they sought to move more deeply in their own lives into holiness of living; they were fervent in prayer; they taught and brought converts together for Bible study, prayer, mutual instruction and witness, and also love feasts. They preached at "Big Meetings" and campmeetings in which there were singing and many expressions of emotions, as people responded happily to their newly converted state.

Primarily the Otterbein-Albright followers moved among the German-speaking persons. There is evidence that they sought to minister to the needs of the poor. Otterbein himself was chosen to be the intermediary for the distribution of clothes and other items to the poor during his pastorate in Baltimore. "When his congregation in Baltimore built a larger, finer parsonage, he preferred to continue to live ... in the little four-roomed building he loved so well and asked that the rental of the new house be given to the poor. When they brought him material for a new suit, he gave it to a poor man across the street."[15]

Perhaps today the Otterbein-Albright tradition could bring new life into our own evangelism. If we could capture the overflowing joy and effusive energy of the heartwarming experience of Christ—the assurance of salvation—there would come such an urgency to share the gospel in deed and word, that the world would believe. For everyone there is the question, "What is your only comfort, in life and in death?" The answer which makes the spirit sing is,

> That I belong—body and soul, in life and in death—not to myself but to my faithful Savior, Jesus Christ, who at the cost of his own blood has fully paid for all my sins and has completely freed me from the dominion of the devil; that he protects me so well that without the will of my Father in heaven not a hair can fall from my head; indeed, that everything must fit his purpose for my salvation. Therefore, by his Holy Spirit, he also assures me of eternal life, and makes me wholeheartedly willing and ready from now on to live for him.[16]

The Otterbein-Albright tradition calls us to such living!

PART TWO

Church

THE GIFTS HE GAVE were that some would be apostles, some prophets, some evangelists, some pastors and teachers, to equip the saints for the work of ministry, for building up the body of Christ, until all of us come to the unity of the faith, and of the knowledge of the Son of God, to maturity, to the measure of the full stature of Christ.

Ephesians 4:11-13

WILLIAM RASPBERRY, a columnist for the *Washington Post*, laments the church's persistence in missing its primary mission. The strategy of good basketball, he writes, has little room for seven-foot giants "playing small": "And still the church, like a seven-foot-tall basketball player shooting jump shots, persists in playing away from its strength—its potential for spiritual regeneration."

Bishop Edwin C. Boulton

CHAPTER 4

Evangelism by All God's People

Ann B. Sherer

WHO ARE THE LAITY? Are they earnest seekers who want to grow up in the spirit and live a life of discipleship in the world? Are they church shoppers, customers, who want a specific set of excellent services? Are they comfortable benchwarmers who come out of habit because they have friends here or want to get to know people? Are they persons who have little interest in dogma but are seeking friends and an accepting community? Are they people who feel the need for a quiet centering time at least once a week? Are they people who feel empty and desire some emotional and spiritual stimulation? Are they persons who hunger and thirst after righteousness? Are they persons who feel that the church offers avenues of meaningful service? Are they persons seeking position, power, and status? Are they persons seeking answers to hard questions in their personal and communal lives? Are they hurt and broken and in need of healing? Are they capable, happy, and desirous of giving back to others some of the bounty they have received? Are they frightened and dogmatic and ready to pick a fight with the first person who disagrees with them? Are they practicing the spiritual disciplines and growing in faith? Are they avid prayers and readers who are actively moving into the depth and breadth of the Christian faith? Are they motivated to serve because of the grace of God which they have experienced?

The *laos*, the people of God, are all there and more. They differ radically. Seeking, running, leading, serving, needing, taking, giving, growing in faith, searching—they come into the community of the church at every place along the faith development spectrum with radically different needs and expectations. Yet Doug Johnson is not far off the mark when he suggests this diverse people is looking for a church that "can assist in their search for deeper religious meanings in their own lives, can guide them in using their time and skills to help others, and can provide them with a network of other people who can support and care for them during some of life's sharpest moments."[1]

The description of the journey of faith based on work by the Saddleback Community Church is especially helpful.[2] This schema suggests several concentric circles of persons living together in community: *seekers, attenders, followers, disciples, apostles*. The *seekers* are those who come to check out the Christian church: to ask questions; experiment with worship; try out various ideas, expressions, and feelings about the faith; sample what the church has to offer them to solve life's problems. Some *seekers* become *attenders* and others become *followers*. *Attenders* come occasionally and want to share in community and worship when there is a felt need, when it is convenient, or when a ministry is offered which they want. Some attenders want to be baptized and allowed to remain on the periphery until they choose to move closer. *Followers* make a decision to follow Jesus. They want to be baptized, enter into the community, and learn how to "walk the walk and talk the talk." They come to worship fairly regularly, join a Sunday School class or some other small group, and take part in a committee or ministry. *Disciples* want to move deeper and let Christ's claim on their lives be primary. In our tradition, they take a Disciple Bible study or commit to some other serious study plan. They want to be part of a small group that holds them responsible for ordering their lives in ways that both nurture them along the Christian way and hold them accountable for living the disciplines of prayer, Bible study, participation in worship and the Holy Sacrament, Christian conference, doing good, refraining from evil. They want to grow up in holiness. *Apostles* continue in a structure of nurture and accountability, but they are pushed beyond the church structures into the world to be in ministry. They know their primary work is not in the church but in the world relating to the hurts and needs of all God's children, sharing the faith, binding up the wounds of the brokenhearted, loving the unlovely, housing the homeless, visiting the prisons, extending the reign of God's love, mercy, righteousness, justice, and grace, sharing in the ministry of reconciliation, sharing with outsiders the joy and promise of the Christian faith. Howard Snyder calls these apostles "kingdom people":

> No church gets in trouble whenever it thinks it is in the church business rather than the Kingdom business . . . Church people think about how to get people into the church; Kingdom people think about how to get the church into the world. Church people worry that the world might change the church; Kingdom people work to see that the church changes the world.[3]

The above schema is consistent with my experience in the church and, perhaps, with the Wesleyan notion of growing in holiness. In baptism God is bound to God's people through a covenant promise, and the people in response are bound to God as they promise to be faithful. As Henry Knight notes,

> both sides of this relationship are necessary to becoming and being a Christian. We are brought into a relationship with God through God's gracious activity, being made partakers of that salvation which God has accomplished in Jesus Christ. Baptism is our initiation into Christ, the assurance of God's faithfulness to all that has been promised through Christ. . . ."[4]

It is the beginning of a lifelong journey which invites and provokes faithful participation in this covenant which God offers and is made tangible in the life of the covenant community of the church. It is a living out of a response to God's love made known in Christ and manifested in baptism. It is the formation of persons who grow in capacity to love and serve God and neighbor. That formation is nurtured as persons avail themselves of the means of grace which God so freely offers in the nurturing and accountable community of the church.

Evangelism, a generous sharing of what they have found of Christ or, better, having been found by Christ, is the work of all God's people—seekers, followers, disciples, and apostles. Wherever people are in this journey of faith God offers opportunities to share what they know, what is real in their life, how the faith is impacting them. "God entrusts evangelism, church planting and cross-cultural mission to all disciples and not just the religious professionals."[5] But of course, it does not always look the same. Where persons are in their journey and the nature of the claim God has on their life determines what people have to share and how they share it.

Similarly, persons differ in temperament. What seems like a generous sharing of experience to one person feels like overwhelming pressure and disrespect for personal boundaries to another. There is no one size which fits all styles for evangelism. Expressions of faith are as diverse as personalities are diverse. And not just personalities. Culture, national origin, gender, economic class, and education contribute to individuality. Out of that individuality comes the sharing of the faith and community experience.

Theological perspective also makes a difference. If a particular theological perspective becomes synonymous with evangelism then only those who occupy that place on the theological spectrum feel any claim on their lives to share generously their faith. Worse still the whole concept of evangelism can be dismissed as the realm of Jerry Falwell and Jim Baker. And others who have a vital faith with different theological content maintain an embarrassed silence about the bedrock of their life rather than risk being identified with a theological position which is not their own.

Given the differences in theology, in personality and life experience, and in places along the Christian journey, how can the diverse community of United Methodism talk about evangelism in a way that invites this diverse community—the *laos*—to share generously the faith that sustains their lives. Rather audaciously, I suggest some general principles.

(1) *Share from a passionate perspective.* The faith perspective is not focused and directed in the same way in all persons. Unless, however, persons have had an emotional or intellectual encounter with God and the faith community which matters deeply to them, having anything to share is indeed difficult.

A recent newsletter article by Barbara Wendland[6] reminds us of Eldon Trueblood's *The Incendiary Fellowship*, a thirty-year-old call to vital faith. He describes the New Testament church as a place where the fiery power of the Holy Spirit burns and people are energized by the spirit to live lives of committed discipleship and shared a faith marked by burning conviction. He suggests that what now passes for Christianity is more vague goodwill than burning conviction. "Though the New Testament describes a hot fire," he says, "we prefer the damp wick."[7]

He warns that the church will not be brought back to life by the "rearrangement of the lives of uncommitted people" or by official pronouncements. Instead persons have to catch on fire. When they experience the power of God's transforming love, the joy of covenant community, and the reality of a new life informed by a story that reveals and makes possible alternative scripts, they have something to share. Trueblood is correct: "The only adequate evidence that anything is on fire is that other fires are started by it . . . A fire that does not spread must eventually go out."[8]

It is self-evident that what individuals have experienced with Jesus Christ and in the community of faith determines what they have to share. In his call to build vital churches, Doug Johnson says: "Vital churches have a message about Jesus Christ's love and life that members can't contain within themselves. Members of vital churches have an excitement about their lives and their faith commitments that grip others. They become activists in the faith. These attributes are attractive to many persons who have been without the church for a long time. They see the vitality of the church members and want to share in whatever it is that turns those people on."[9]

(2) *Share from a sense of God's call*. The call to share the good news of God's love is rooted in the awareness that God is a loving, seeking God who has been reaching out to humankind since creation. The biblical witness is the story of God's beckoning persons through the biblical narrative of Abraham and Sarah, the offer of a covenant relationship, the Exodus, the law, the prophets, Jesus the Christ, the Holy Spirit, the church. That humankind is broken and in need of God's love and redemption is as real as the daily newspaper or a glance inside the self. The lengths God will go are evident in the cross. When persons accept the gift of God's love and become part of the covenant community God invites those persons to share in God's redemptive, loving work by acts of mercy, love, justice, and kindness and by telling others what one knows about the God who acts and how God acts. "Faith sharing is founded in the love of God."[10]

(3) *Share out of personal experience*. That does not mean all sharing of the faith is inviting others to focus on one's life and experience, but it does mean "giving evidence on which we are willing to stake our lives" and "allowing the word of God to live in one's heart and show forth in one's life."[11] Outsiders often think the worst of religion and are helped not by triumphalism but by the witness of searching questions in the presence of God. Those without all the answers are often the most helpful. George Hunter suggests that the best persons to reach secular people are fellow travelers, who "share out of the ups and downs of their life and faith."[12]

The Word has to become flesh in people. It is through personality that truth gets communicated. In the early church people experienced God's reality in the risen, living Christ and they shared that with others. On the eve of the twenty-first century persons are still called to share the way the good news impacts their life. Faith sharing is telling what God is doing in one's life. Fox and Morris offer the reminder that lifestyle and quality of life affect the capacity to be a credible witness to that gospel.[13]

Evangelism understood in this way is radical activity by a person who has been radically changed. Brueggemann pushes this edge:

> Evangelism . . . is an activity of transformed consciousness that results in an altered perception of world, neighbor, and self, and an authorization to live differently in that world. The news that God has triumphed means that a transformed life, i.e., one changed by the hearing of the news, works to bring more and more of life, personal and public, under the rule of this world-transforming, slave-liberating, covenant-making, promise-keeping, justice-commanding God.[14]

(4) *Listen to people and their stories of hope and pain.* Whether the field is business or industry or church or government planning, the plethora of how-to books nudges persons to listen, to take the time to hear the hurts and needs and hopes and dreams of people. As a byproduct of the individualization of the American culture, people are lonely and unrelated, in desperate need for someone to hear and care about what is happening to them and within them.

(5) *Relate to persons with genuine appreciation for the other person.* Some of the descriptions of relational evangelism are overtly manipulative. In a seminar I attended several years ago a speaker told how he won a person for Christ. He had a neighbor who was not a Christian and he wanted to share the faith with him. He knew that this neighbor liked frog-gigging and so he started going frog-gigging with him until he joined the church. I felt an uneasiness. If the evangelist genuinely cared for the other and continued to care and spend time with him after he joined the church then I celebrate this faith sharing. If the caring stops when the commitment is made everyone is the loser. If the motive of the evangelist is primarily something other than caring about what is happening to another, then the dangers loom. More than one cynic echoes James Adams' words:

> The great interest in evangelism appears to come not out of concern for human beings who live without hope but out of an anxiety about dwindling numbers. The more church membership declines as a percentage of the population, the more interest church leaders

show in evangelism. In each of the major denominations, the factions promoting evangelism seem to have convinced the policy-makers that they know how to save the church from a continuing decline in membership.[15]

Institutional maintenance is not a good enough reason for persons to reach out to others to share the good news. But when people share with another because they care about the other and want to include them in on how God has enriched their lives, then the fire spreads. Because of this relational factor, persons who are invited to church like to sit with those who invited them. They value these persons calling to check on them, calling to see how they felt about the church experience. This feels normal and natural. A calling committee, on the other hand, feels institutional and impersonal. George Barna urges this kind of personal follow-up.[16]

(6) *Motivated by a concern for the well-being of persons, relate to the needs and concerns of the individual.* We need to recognize that we have different gifts and different experiences of faith. If I allow another to share his or her gift without censure and am given the same freedom, persons from many walks of life can hear the life-transforming news. The good news does not always sound the same from every witness. Because brokenness varies, so does the healing.

In 1986 when I became superintendent of the Nacogdoches District, Texas Conference, the local NOW group asked me to come and speak, primarily because I was a woman in a nontraditional role. Fifty or sixty women were packed into the small space of the Yakofritz Sandwich Shop, with its bare floors and poster-lined walls. I told them a little about superintending and the role of women in The United Methodist Church. Then the questions began. Most of the women had grown up in the church, but none had attended a church for more than a year. As far as they knew there was no connection between feminism and Christianity. When I talked about inclusive language, read from an inclusive language lectionary, shared the Social Principles, they wanted to know more. Over forty women stayed until almost midnight. They were spiritually hungry and eager to know more about a faith stance that affirmed their own understanding of the value and equality of women. I was able to let outsiders know one of the places where the Christian faith had offered me a gift and might offer them one as well.

Christianity is usually spread not by dramatic stranger-to-stranger encounters but through normal social networks of family, common interests, or work. And the telling of the story is shaped by the context and the life experience of the speaker and the listener.

(7) *Use language that communicates.* Don't begin by explaining "churchy" concepts. George Hunter talks of people being "ignostic"—that is, they simply do not know what the church is talking about with its insider language and intramural debates.

(8) *Recognize that this is the post-Christian era.* The United States of America is a secular society. Most of the populous profess a vague belief in God but less than half are actively involved in any faith community and believe that faith makes a claim on their life. If invited to church by a stranger, at least half of the persons between the ages of twenty-five and forty-five would say, "I do not do church." Many of these persons have not been involved in church. They do not know the stories. And what they think they know about the church is often negative: moralistic, condemning, arrogant are words that they use to describe the church.

About a year ago I visited Cox Hospital in Springfield, Missouri. I was amazed to discover this 350-bed hospital had five chaplains. When asked about this high chaplain/patient ratio, they gave an answer that surprised me. Springfield, with an Assemblies of God seminary and several church-related colleges, is assumed to be the buckle on the Bible Belt. They took a survey of patients. Less than half could give both a religious preference and a pastor's name. A hospital population is skewed toward the older adult population who are more active in the church, and yet even so, less than half of them had enough of a relationship with the church to know a pastor's name. This data gives a rather strong witness that secularization is part of life, even in Springfield, Missouri.

(9) *Gain knowledge.* The sociology, psychology, and theology of the church is well-documented. Knowledge is essential if clergy and laity are going to be partners in making disciples, in reaching out to the community. How does the small church work? Read Carl Dudley and Douglas Walrath's *Developing Your Small Church's Potential*.[17] How might family systems theory be applied to the church? Read Edwin Friedman's *Generation to Generation*.[18] What might it mean to be the church in a secular society? Read Loren Mead's *The Once and Future Church*[19] or George Hunter's *How To Reach Secular People*.[20] The list goes on.

Gain knowledge by listening to the people around you. What are they saying about where they hurt, what they need, what they hope?

What resources of time, money, and talent are available within you, within the church? Where is the church meeting human hurt and need and where are the gaps?

(10) *Know that God's vision is inclusive.* It may be true, as some church growth experts suggest, that it is easier for the church to attract people like the ones they already have. Certainly it is important for those persons to hear how God and church make a difference. But the object is not just growing a church. It is telling and being the good news, making disciples and apostles, being ones God can use in the transformation of the whole world.

The last church I served before entering the episcopacy was Westbury United Methodist Church in Houston, Texas. More than thirty nationalities worshiped together. There was an Ibo Choir made up of persons from Nigeria. There were Hispanic, African, African American, and Asian persons, as well as many with European background, who served on the Board or taught a class. The church was 30 percent non-white and new persons of every race were entering the congregation weekly. When needs are recognized and met, when there is a deep concern for persons and they can easily find ways to relate to others, when people are invited to give themselves away, when worship is joyous and vital, people join a multicultural congregation. One caveat. Class differences are harder to overcome than racial differences, but it is possible if the church listens well and acts with compassion. Tex Sample's *Hard Living People and Mainstream Christians* offers some ways to sharpen listening skills and to develop a compassionate heart.[21]

The *laos*, the diverse people of God, can generously let outsiders, another diverse people, in on what they have found of value in Christianity. When evangelism is defined as generosity, the covenant community is reminded that hospitality is a mark of the followers of Jesus and everyone—*seeker, attender, follower, disciple, apostle*—is welcome in the theologically and culturally diverse faith community. This hospitality is made known through ministries that address the hurts and needs of insiders and outsiders. This hospitality is made known "when members of the church are so convinced that God has enriched their lives through their participation in the life of a Christian community that they want to include other people in what they have found to be valuable."[22] This hospitality is made known when persons have a passion for the faith, know God's consistent caring for humankind, speak out of personal experience, listen to others and relate genuinely to them, understand the secular culture and use language that communicates, and seek sociological, psychological, theological, and systemic knowledge that enables effective listening, planning, and speaking.

At Pentecost the Spirit of God came to the whole people of God giving them power to bear witness to Jesus Christ. All of God's people are ministers of Jesus Christ and called to share the good news of God. Each can share his or her own peculiar story, witness, and ministry. God continues to call, shape, nurture, and send God's own people and to entrust to them the message that has the power to make individuals and the world whole. Wherever persons are on that journey with God, they can generously share with others what they have found of value in the faith. Central to the Christian life is faith sharing.

CHAPTER 5

The United Methodist Church as Evangelist

Richard B. Wilke

THE THIRTY-YEAR DECLINE of our denomination has produced a plethora of books and articles analyzing our plight. When I wrote *And Yet We Are Alive* about a decade ago, I was merely offering a journalistic scream in the night. It has now been accompanied by a host of diagnostic insights by some of our best theologians and church thinkers. But our beloved church, like a dying man, probed, punched, x-rayed, and examined by a phalanx of physicians, does not get well by description or diagnosis. In fact, the patient may get worse by the handling and by the exposure to the cold air.

Little has changed. The decline of The United Methodist Church in the U.S., in numerical strength and influence, continues unchecked and unabated. Hints of recovery have proven to be mere moments of unrealistic optimism. The numerical losses are now less because the size of the church is smaller, but the percentage of loss stays about the same. Our corporate age is ten to fifteen years more than that of the population as a whole. We bury more than we baptize. We have more funerals than conversions. Even the flagship of our fleet, the United Methodist Women, has diminished from over one and a half million members to less than a million. In three decades we have closed between four and five thousand churches while opening less than a thousand new ones.

Disclaimers are shouted from every corner. Some say we shouldn't air our dirty linen in public or even talk about negative things, so they hurry to discuss other, mostly irrelevant, matters. Others treat statistics as naughty words and accounting as if it were an ignoble task. They always audit the money meticulously but imply that people are not important enough to be counted. They say they do not want a "Methodist Statistical Church" where we play a "numbers game." Neither do I. But people have names, and they can be counted whether they are present or absent. Still others refuse to be caught trying to "save the institution," downplaying the role of people who spend their lives trying to save a business, a university, or a government. They have a point, however, for God surely does have a purpose more divine for Methodism than merely trying to save itself.

Beware of those who twist every appeal for evangelization into a plan for church growth or institutional survival. Our founder declared that we have "nothing to do but to save souls," a dream far more divine than institutional preservation. Most feeble of all, however, are "damn the torpedoes, full speed ahead" commentators who insist that we must be faithful to our erstwhile convictions and our current ideologies as if we were martyrs in our present course of action. Sometimes the church has been smaller and more faithful, as when Wesley kicked backsliders out of his class meetings, but it hardly describes our current condition. We are not declining because we are faithful to the commands of our Lord.

In our private moments, we know that we are, to use Søren Kierkegaard's phrase, "sick unto death." In guarded conversations, we acknowledge that we have lost our focus, that we are burdened with bureaucracy, that we have politicized our witness. We sense that we have drifted from our biblical moorings and that we are out of touch with the masses of people. We know that we have become an upper middle-class church. Bishop Kenneth Carder has warned us that we have actualized John Wesley's fear: that Methodist convictions would lead sober, hard-working, frugal people to worldly success, ending in presumptive self-sufficiency and independence.[1] One bureaucrat was quoted in *Time* a few years ago: "Don't be afraid, the bishops will keep the money rolling in."

Many sociological causes for our decline have been calibrated. The dramatic deterioration of rural America where The Evangelical United Brethren and Methodist Churches were once so strong is a far-reaching reality. Thousands of towns and villages, once teeming with children and youth who overcrowded our Sunday schools, have long since dried up. Our sprawling urbanization fills the streets with Hispanics, African Americans, rural poor, immigrants from all over the world. The vast majority is totally unchurched. Cultural

Catholics, Jews, and Muslims flood the cities and confuse us. Our work and witness in the metropolitan areas has been pitifully weak. The U.S. population is now 261 million—a net gain of 2.5 million last year alone. About 97 percent of the population lives in the cities, and, except for a community center here and a suburban church there, we stand bewildered.

Politically we are categorized by the news media with the "L" word. We are often identified with the political left as if we were a political party. They might be amazed at who we really are if they polled the total membership, but as Albert Outler insisted, if we become a political entity, then, when political winds shift, we shall be left in the side-drifts of history.

Into this world of self-criticism and numerical decline, we come asking, like Nicodemus, "What must we do to be saved?" How can we become God's evangelist once again? For an evangelistic agent we once were! We must never forget, as George Hunter has reminded us, that in Wesley's time England was parceled out in parishes.[2] The entire country was marked off like graph paper with every nook and cranny, every living soul included in a parish, every parish with a church, and every church with a priest. There was no need for the Methodist revival save one—most of the people were baptized but unsaved. Currently, we still practice baptism, but much of our practice is a romantic attempt to hold to the form when the Spirit is leaving. Most of England's working peasants and most of the industrialized poor lived outside the faith and fellowship of the church, so God raised up the Wesleyan revival.

We can never forget that Methodism is an evangelical movement, born on the streets when a cathedral already stood on the corner. We were an evangelistic movement on the eastern seaboard of the U.S. when churches were already well-established. After the Civil War, Methodism raced westward with unbridled enthusiasm into uncharted territory, shouting, in the words of C. C. McCabe's telegram to Bob Ingersall, "All Hail the Power of Jesus's Name—we are building one Methodist church for every day of the year, and propose to make it two a day!"[3]

But more than that, we can never forget the command of our Savior. Mortimer Arias has pointed out that each of the four Gospels ends with a unique form of the great commission.[4] In John's Gospel, Jesus tells Peter to pull in his net of fish—exactly one hundred fifty-three of them (the total number of species of fish listed in the scientific journals of the day—a symbol for the entire world)—and then tells Peter "feed my sheep." Luke ends his first volume with Jesus appearing on the road to Emmaus, then joining the disciples to say, "Thus it is written, that the Messiah is to suffer and to rise from the dead on the third day, and that repentance and forgiveness of sins is to be proclaimed in his name to all nations" (Luke 24:46-47). Mark, with many manuscripts tattered at the end, invariably includes a commission. The shorter ending reads "Jesus himself sent out through them, from east to west, the sacred and imperishable proclamation of eternal salvation" (Mark 16:8*b*). Matthew is best known: "Go therefore and make disciples of all nations, baptizing them in the name of the Father and of the Son and of the Holy Spirit, and teaching them to obey everything that I have commanded you" (Matt. 28:19-20).

Thus, certain that we are on the right track, the key question becomes, How can we break out of our lethargy? How can we get our priorities straight? How can we shake off the barnacles from our boat, and be obedient to that "first love" to which John referred in the Revelation? Can an entire denomination be born again? Can American Methodism enter again into its mother's womb? Where can we go for guidance? I want to suggest Paul's Epistle to the Romans, for two reasons.

First, Dietrich Bonhoeffer, in *The Cost of Discipleship*, insists that "revival of church life always brings in its train a richer understanding of the Scriptures."[5] He also argues that church life is renewed as we listen clearly and cleanly to the Scriptures. His attack on cheap grace uses Luther's deep understanding of Romans as its basis. In fact church history confirms that almost every great revival of the church is grounded in a fresh discovery of Romans: Augustine, Luther, Calvin, Wesley, Kierkegaard, Karl Barth.

Second, not only is a rediscovery of Romans vital for rebirth, but the latest scholarship makes it exciting as well. Dr. Leander Keck, distinguished New Testament Professor, demonstrates this in an essay entitled, "What Makes Romans Tick?"[6] Keck shines a spotlight on the seldom-studied fifteenth chapter to understand why Paul wrote Romans in the first place. He had never been to Rome. He had slept in the homes of Thessalonica, sung hymns in the jail in Philippi, made tents and preached in Corinth, but Rome's church he did not start and had never visited. So he writes, "I have written to you rather boldly" (unsolicited, actually) "because of the grace given me by

God" (now watch) "to be a minister of Christ to the *Gentiles*. . . . I will not venture to speak of anything except what Christ has accomplished through me to win obedience from the *Gentiles*" (15:15-18, emphasis added). Some of Paul's readers are Jewish converts. What is happening? He goes on to build his case: "From Jerusalem and as far around as Illyricum I have fully proclaimed the good news of Christ" (he has worked the eastern end of the Mediterranean). "Thus I make it my ambition to proclaim the good news, not where Christ has already been named, so that I do not build on someone else's foundation." Then he quotes the prophet Isaiah, "Those who have never been told of him shall see, and those who have never heard of him shall understand." He drives his position home, "now, with no further place for me in these regions, I desire, as I have for many years, to come to you *when I go to Spain*." (I always thought the apostle wanted to go to Rome, but Rome was to be only a stopover; Spain was his ultimate destination!) Listen, "for I do hope to see you on my journey and to be sent on by you, once I have enjoyed your company for a little while" (15:20-24, emphasis added).

What was Paul doing when he wrote to Rome? He was fulfilling his vow to Peter and James to gather money for the martyred poor Jewish Christians in Jerusalem. The covenant made at the Council of Jerusalem was that in exchange for their blessing to take the gospel to the uncircumcised Gentiles, Paul would teach converts not to drink blood, to avoid sexual immorality, and to collect money for the ravaged poor in Judea. So Paul was traveling through Greece, shoring up his young churches, gathering the offering, and fulfilling that chapter of his ministry.

He had to take the money to Jerusalem personally because his integrity was at stake. But more important, the unity of the church hung in balance. Could Jewish Christians and Gentile Christians hold together? Would Christianity be merely a Jewish sect? Or would Gentile Christianity flourish, rid itself of Jewish roots, and become another Graeco-Roman religion? When Paul placed the money at Peter's feet, the bond between Jew and Gentile, brought together by the blood of Christ, would be ratified. The Jewish mother had given birth to the church through suffering. Now the Gentile children would pour back sacrificial love in return. The mission to the world would be secure.

Paul's mission had been centered in Ephesus. We tend to think of Paul always on the go. That is the spirit of the book of Acts. We study "Paul's missionary journeys." But Paul stayed about three years in Ephesus, the major Roman city in the Eastern Mediterranean. He rented a downtown school room, lecturing at noon or in the evening. He dispatched a flood of emissaries: Timothy to Philippi; Titus to Corinth; Epaphrus to Laodicea, Hierapolis, and Colossae. In short, when Paul hugged and kissed the converts on the shore near Ephesus he was not only saying a personal farewell, he was leaving behind his base of operations for the entire eastern end of the Mediterranean. He was preparing to establish a similar base of operations in the West, in Rome, so that he could evangelize Spain.

Why Spain? It was the last country on the map. Maps of the day showed dragons in the uncharted seas of the Atlantic. To go to Spain would fulfill the Lord's command "that repentance and forgiveness of sins is to be proclaimed in his name to all nations" (Luke 24:47). But Spain was also virgin territory for the gospel, almost totally devoid of Judaism, a Gentile world. Paul wrote, "Thus I make it my ambition to proclaim the good news, not where Christ has already been named, so that I do not build on someone else's foundation" (Rom. 15:20).

Paul needed several things from the Roman Christians. He needed them to know that he was an authentic apostle, grounded in the Scriptures, called by Jesus Christ who was raised from the dead, and dedicated "to bring about the obedience of faith among all the Gentiles" (Rom. 1:5). Second, he needed a harmonious fellowship; Jewish and Gentile Christian would need to be of one mind, thus his long discussion of obedient faith descending from Abraham and Sarah. Third, he must have relationships of love and prayer. That is why he wrote, "I remember you always in my prayers" (1:10) and asked them to be "in earnest prayer to God on my behalf" as he approached Jerusalem (15:31). That is why he mentioned twenty-six colleagues and friends in the greetings, including Phoebe, the deacon who was to carry and interpret the letter. Fourth, they must know and affirm his missional strategy. But most significant of all, they must know in their minds, understand in their hearts, and authenticate in their lives, the gospel. "For I am not ashamed of the gospel; it is the power of God for salvation to everyone who has faith, to the Jew first and also to the Greek" (1:16). What makes Romans tick is that Paul had to articulate to the Roman Christians, in careful detail, the good news he would carry to Spain. That delineation has come to us, and it is the power of God unto salvation for us as well.

What is this gospel? We must say it straight out, for it is not being pronounced from many of our United Methodist pulpits. It begins with the wrath of God, that holiness of God which burns collectively against the wickedness of humankind. When was the last sermon we preached on the wrath of God? Some religious educators and pastors criticized the Disciple Bible Study for allowing the prophets of Israel to suggest that God punishes people for their sins. Wrath is not capricious anger, like lightening scorching a sinner from some supernatural cloud. Wrath is goodness offended by evil, harmony weeping over broken relations, compassion recoiling at hatred, truth insisting on being found out. Wrath stands over against our corporate and personal sin, condemning it and ultimately destroying it, for "the wages of sin are death." The message of the prophet Habakkuk was that the greedy can never rest, that those who shame their friends will be shamed in return, that violence will beget violence, that a city built on blood will not stand (cf. Hab. 2:12-17). Our God of wrath gives the disobedient up to their own passions.

Sin is our grabbing control of our lives, breaking the holy laws of God, corporately and individually, fracturing relationships, and, as Paul said, "serving the creature rather than the Creator." Paul understood that we are tyrannized by that power. Like a ship boarded by pirates, our minds have been taken over by an enslaving power. Sin is, for the gospel, an alien tyrant, sitting in the control room of our hearts. More tragic still, that power has a kingdom-like quality. We are all caught in a web of wickedness, enslaved into a corporate reign of self-centeredness. There is no need to judge others. There is enough guilt go around, enough wrath for everybody. "God shows no partiality" (Rom. 2:11). Antinomianism has all but destroyed our understanding of sin. Most of our people think of sin as individual mistakes or transgressions; the gospel understands sin as the tragic broken relationship between humankind and God. Further, sin and wrath are not limited to humankind. Especially in our times we should know that sin ravages the land, contaminates the streams, and pollutes the atmosphere. The whole universe is infected with sin and wrath.

Paul wants them to understand the law, the law of Moses and the inner law of conscience. The integrity of God is at stake. Was the law bad? "By no means" (Rom. 7:7). The law is not our real problem; sin is our real problem. I grew up reading the ten commandments from the hymnal as we took Holy Communion. Today, I never hear the commandments read, and I do not find them in the communion ritual. The law is holy, for it reflects the righteousness of God and reveals the nature of right relationships. But it did not save. What does sin do when faced by the rules? Sin rebels more. Tell a child not to touch a hot stove and what does the child do? He or she quickly reaches out to touch the stove. Tell a teenager not to play around in the back seat and he or she leaves the dance early. Paul says that sin "seized the opportunity." So the law, wise as a parent's counsel, fair as a speed limit, does not have the power to overcome sin, to bring us into a right relationship with our loving God. The failure of the law is not that it is incorrect, but that it lacks power to root out sin. The old idol of self-seeking must be replaced. A new resident must move into the human heart (cf. Rom. 8:17). So God, in faithful compassion, has acted again: "God has done what the law ... could not do, by sending his own son in the likeness of sinful flesh ... so that the requirement of the law might be fulfilled in us" (8:3-4). The obedient love of Christ even unto death undoes the legacy of self-centeredness lingering since Adam. The resurrection of Jesus confirms and ratifies his victory over all principalities and powers, especially the last enemy, death itself. Pope John Paul puts it this way, "Indestructible life, revealed in the Resurrection of Christ, 'swallows,' so to speak, death."[7] "Where, O death, is your victory?", asks the apostle Paul, with his eyes fixed on the risen Christ (1 Cor. 15:55). All evangelization revolves around the cross.

Paul suggests that the believer leaves one form of slavery (a slavery of self that leads to death) and enters a new form of slavery (a slavery in Christ that leads to life). The Christian believer accepts both the active mode and the passive mode of faith, as E. Stanley Jones, our greatest evangelist of this century has shown us.[8] The active mode obeys the command of Jesus, "Come and follow me." The passive mode obeys the command of Jesus, "Wait until the Holy Spirit comes upon you." I obeyed the first command when I was fifteen. But when I was introduced to Romans in seminary, I began to understand our Lord's unconditional grace. The first response accepts him as *Savior*; the second response accepts him as *Lord*.

For Paul the death of Christ is accompanied by the death of the soul of the believer. The resurrection of Christ is lived out in the resurrection of the believer from sin and fear of death. Surrendered human souls, dead to self and risen in Christ, live in Christ and Christ lives in them. That Holy Spirit, that Spirit of Jesus, is communal and only communal. One does not experience the Spirit, then live in isolation. To be "in Christ" is to be a part of the reconciliation, to live expecting the coming harmonies of God with sisters and brothers of faith, to set one's mind "on the Spirit in life and peace [Shalom]." Then comes the mighty "therefore" of Romans 12, in which we are to live out collectively the work of Christ's body, sustaining one another in forgiving love, and offering the gospel and our righteous just dealings and kindness to the world until our Lord comes again in all-consuming glory. For Paul, no other choices exist. We either live to ourselves, apart from God, broken in our relationships, at war with ourselves, or we live together in quiet obedient trust, bearing witness to the gospel which is the power of our salvation. "All who are led by the Spirit of God are the children of God" (Rom. 8:14). We are not yet fully saved, "for in hope we were saved" (8:24). So we wait expectantly, not "waiting for Godot," but waiting for the One we know and love. We are weak so we bind together, always reaching out to the disoriented, as a sailor on a life raft might reach out to another drowning sailor. And always we are groaning with the whole creation, waiting for a new heaven and a new earth, praying "Come, Lord Jesus."

We are well advised to draw upon Paul's letter to the Romans to help us learn of the new life in Christ. What can we do to be once again the evangelistic movement we were called to be?

(1) *Do we know where the Gentiles are?* I listen to the prayers in church. We pray for people with cancer, yet we seldom pray for the kids on the street who as God said to Jonah, "don't know their right hand from their left." Many of them are poor, single mothers with children. They don't know the Apostles' Creed or the Gloria Patri. They sing about drugs and darkness, about the devil and death. Why do we not pray for them? As a Korean bishop said at our General Conference, "I hear your prayers, but I do not see your tears." We must go to the Gentiles. Stop everything else and go to the Gentiles.

(2) *Do we know how little time there is?* Since what we are doing is leading to the death of the church, let us stop doing what we are doing. We church executives waste our lives in endless housekeeping meetings. Our pastor's hold the hands of the parishioners, spending 95 percent of their hours with the faithful. Who is left to teach the Gentiles? The only people left are a few recent converts who will talk to their friends. Our energies must be reallocated.

(3) *Have we examined our structures?* If they are not designed to

carry the gospel, we should abandon them. It is amazing how fast a bureau will close if it is not funded, how fast a commission will die if no one attends. Be positive. Spend so much time and energy teaching the poor and the poor in spirit about the Savior that the whole church will have no time left for meetings in which no one is saved. The meeting in Jerusalem lasted only a few days, but it launched a lifetime of mission.

(4) *When we go to the Gentiles, are we prepared to take the gospel?* The real gospel, the full gospel? Can we preach wrath and sin and atonement and surrendered obedient faith to a risen Savior? As Pope John Paul II wrote, "the whole world revolves around the cross."[9] Can we preach, as John Wesley tried to do, the saving power of Christ in every sermon? Can we say with Paul "I am not ashamed of the gospel; it is the power of God for salvation" (Rom. 1:16)?

(5) *Are we striving after unity?* Do we love one another? Divisions marked the Corinthian church. Racial disharmony, language barriers, and gender discrimination will put a disclaimer to our message of love in Jesus Christ. We will never evangelize our cities with a lily-white middle-class bunch of barriers. The best way to overcome internecine conflict is to fling yourselves into gospel teaching and preaching and to do it together using Jews and Greeks and barbarians, women and men, speaking all the languages on earth. "How very good and pleasant it is when kindred live together in unity! It is like the precious oil on the head, running down upon the beard, on the beard of Aaron" (Ps. 133:1-2). An army on the march has little time to quarrel.

(6) *Do we have a plan?* We need to devise a plan for winning the Gentiles in our land as well as sending missionaries to the far-flung corners of the earth. Remember, Mr. Wesley went most quickly to those farthest from the church. In a letter to Dorothy Furly in 1757, he wrote, "I love the poor, in many of them I find pure, genuine grace, unmixed with paint, folly and affectation."[10] As Bishop Kenneth Carder has stated correctly, "The poor and the marginalized, which is one of the fastest growing segments of the world's population, may be our best hope for the recovery of the message of grace."[11] The best thing the Council of Bishops could do would be to draw apart for a month for prayer and planning, simply and clearly asking the Lord to help us devise a plan for carrying the gospel to the unbelieving world, especially to the physically and spiritually impoverished children and youth of America.

(7) *Are we using all our personnel resources for the conversion of the world?* Thousands of Methodists would teach, preach, and witness if we would let them, if we would free them up. Church leaders often say they need half a million dollars to start a church. Recently we started two churches, both of which cost little. The first was begun by one of our most distinguished retired pastors in a Wesley Foundation building. Now with one hundred and fifty members, it has a full time pastor. A second was begun by a medical doctor sixty-three years of age, who wanted to be a part-time local pastor. He began with a Disciple Bible study group, graduated to a motel, and now meets in an abandoned convent with one hundred eighty in worship. He gives his modest salary back to the church. Volunteers in Mission, squashed by the church as late as twenty years ago, is now an explosive movement that requires almost no official funding. If our members were armed with the gospel and put to work without constraints, they could set the world ablaze.

(8) *Where shall we meet?* Since Pauline Christians had no church buildings, they met in homes. How often Paul would close his letters by sending greetings to the church that met in somebody's house. In our city, the fastest-growing church is a Fellowship Bible church which invites people to a house church before inviting them to Sunday services. They stole that from us. Many Koreans insist that the Wesley class meeting, with weekly training for the leaders and built-in spiritual accountability has led to thousands of conversions. Covenant groups, class meetings, Disciple groups can be as prevalent as we have living rooms. This door is wide open to us. It is our biblical and Wesleyan heritage.

(9) *Why are we not leading?* This is perhaps the most difficult issue. John and Charles Wesley didn't lead by making appointments, they led by preaching, teaching, witnessing. They actually converted people. They actually went to the jails, to the widows, to the kids in the streets. They went personally to the coal mines. Do you remember how hard it was for Mr. Wesley to begin preaching in the open air to the poor? But he did it. And our American pioneer bishop, Francis Asbury? How long did it take him to make his appointments? He was quickly on his horse, preaching more times, singing more hymns, witnessing in more farmhouses than all the rest of them. Remember, Paul didn't ask Timothy to go to Spain. He planned to go himself.

CHAPTER 6

Discipleship and the Evangelistic Task

Bruce P. Blake

FOR THE PAST DECADE, persons referred to as "baby boomers" have been asking a significant question: "Is the church credible?" For the past two or three years, members of what we call "Generation X" have been asking a more significant question: "Is the Christian message credible?" This question is basic to any attempt which endeavors to address the relationship of discipleship and the evangelistic task. Researchers claim that members of Generation X have largely been ignored by established Christian churches. This has happened because the Christian community is not prepared to deal with the question they are raising.

Recently, I was a participant in two experiences during which the latter question was addressed. The first experience was a twenty-four hour retreat with bishops and judicatory executives from several denominations which cover the same geographic area as the North Texas Conference. During this retreat, as this question was addressed and dealt with seriously and personally, a consensus emerged. The message, as typically presented in local congregations, often is not credible. The message, as packaged in the lives of many professing Christians, often is not credible.

The second experience involved a church school class. The subject of the morning was "witnessing." These lay persons clearly made the following points: "If witnessing means I must put another person down or insist that he or she must join me in my faith journey, I want no part of it." "The only witness which has impact is that of the one who has first lived his or her life according to the fruits of the Spirit." "The core of the message must be identified, for the more layers persons have to peel off to discover the core, the more likely it is that the layers and the core will become confused."

These recent experiences provide a backdrop for a consideration of the subject of discipleship and the evangelistic task. Only when we are clear and concise about the message, proclaiming it in words and deeds, without disparaging or judging others, is it experienced as credible.

Discussions and strategies related to the evangelistic task are noisy gongs and clanging cymbals unless the message is clear, concise, and credible. For me, the credible message is the good news that my sins are forgiven! The credible message is that, as a person who has fallen short of God's glory, and who continually misses the mark of God's high calling, I am offered forgiveness by God. When I say "yes" to the gift of forgiveness, revealed in the cross of Christ, I am so full of joy that I share my story of being forgiven with others.

The credible message is Jesus Christ, who is our forgiveness. Forgiveness is the heart of the good news. Forgiveness is the experience of salvation. Forgiveness ushers one into a life of living the fruits of the Spirit. Without forgiveness, faith is negative and full of bad news. On the foundation of Jesus Christ as our forgiveness, faith is affirmative and full of good news. The layers of theology, or additional systems of belief which are added to this credible message, are not the heart and soul of the gospel and must never be confused with it. Forgiveness is the heart and soul of the gospel. In a world where little is forgiven, the radical message of forgiveness is relevant and credible.

In the context of these understandings and convictions I have made three discoveries. First, discipleship and the evangelistic task are two sides of the same coin. Second, the evangelistic task and church growth are not the same. Third, a unique and distinctive mark of United Methodists as evangelists is that the good news is shared in the context of grace, not judgment. These discoveries were not made through reading and research. Rather, they were made as a consequence of walking with God's children, most recently among United Methodists in North Texas and in Africa, among faithful evangelists, disciples of Jesus Christ.

Discipleship and Evangelism

The United Methodist Church and many other denominations have frequently not served the reign of God well. Often, evangelism has fallen by the wayside because the church has communicated that individuals can be disciples by living out one of several expressions of discipleship, of which evangelism is but one optional form. The church and individual Christians now need to understand that one cannot be a disciple of Jesus Christ without being personally involved in the evangelistic task. The evangelistic task is not peripheral to discipleship. Indeed, discipleship and evangelism are inseparable. When one follows Jesus Christ, the journey begins with the experience of forgiveness. A forgiven person follows Christ by witnessing (telling one's story), by praising God (in worship), by growing in grace (through service and education), and by being a suffering servant (through deeds of peace, justice, and mercy).

When I visited Africa in 1992, I learned more about the evangelistic task by observing than I ever imagined possible. One thing I learned was that the evangelistic task in Africa is grounded in a basic belief about God. United Methodists in Africa believe that God has chosen to depend on the church as an instrument of God's mission in the world. They believe this dependence is a part of God's plan, revealed in the Christ event. Their understanding of the Incarnation is that, in Jesus Christ, God announced to the world, "I will share my love through human flesh, in Jesus Christ." They believe that from that event until today, God's love is shared through human beings, through God's church. They believe God is evangelistic through the church. Hence, the church is neither source nor goal of evangelism. The church is the means, and herein is the crucial function of the church. United Methodists believe that just as human beings are dependent upon God, God chooses to depend on human beings. That is the meaning of Christmas; that is the message of the Incarnation. God chooses to be vulnerable by calling the church to voice the good news of forgiveness in Jesus Christ.

In Angola, I continually heard references to a woman who had told her story of faith to many persons. A great number had become church members as a consequence of her witness. On my last day in Angola I met her. I had expected to meet one mature in years, but, instead I found her to be a working mother with two children at home. I said to her, "I have heard about you all week. Tell me, how do you find time to witness and why do you share your story of faith?" She responded with this statement that I will never forget, "God has no voice but my voice." She smiled. I smiled. I asked no more questions.

This is a powerful lesson—to believe that God has chosen that disciples through the church should be the carriers of the good news of Jesus Christ means that God depends on me. This gives power and motivation to the evangelistic task. If a person believes this, he or she will be evangelistic, and vice versa, if a person does not believe this, he or she will not be evangelistic. Simply stated, a commitment to the evangelistic task is dependent on the understanding that God depends on us.

Another lesson I learned in Africa was that there is no probationary period required to be an evangelist. When one becomes a believer, one does not have to be trained, educated, oriented, or incubated in any other way. Once a believer, a person is an evangelist; once a Christian, immediately an evangelist.

Being an evangelist is a part of the rhythm of faith. A person experiences forgiveness and shares his or her story with others. As the story is told, it reinforces the centrality of the experience of forgiveness within Christian life and community. In sharing the story, one is publicly held accountable to a lifestyle based on the ethics of forgiveness. On the other hand, if one does not tell the story, the importance of forgiveness is not known and shared, and the Christian ethic is closeted in privacy. Being a Christian and being private is an impossible marriage. The lesson is plain. Christianity and being an evangelist are inseparable.

In Zimbabwe, I visited a pastor who had been called from his graduate studies in Pennsylvania to become pastor of a congregation which had several hundred in attendance but no pastoral leadership. This congregation said to the bishop, "We have 400–500 in worship on Sunday mornings. Please send us a pastor."

I visited the pastor on a Monday after his fourth Sunday in the pulpit. The attendance had nearly tripled in a month—there had been 1,400 people in worship. I asked him how this had happened. He replied that at the conclusion of his first worship service, which was a wonderful experience of faith, he asked the congregation if it had been a good experience. "Yes," was the reply. He asked if they had experienced God's grace. "Yes," they answered. He then asked them to think of a neighbor, family member, friend, or co-worker whom they knew was not in church. There was silence. Then he asked them to go to that person during the week and share with him or her about their experiences in Christian worship. In four weeks, attendance nearly tripled. Why? Because persons were expected to be evangelists without meeting any probationary time requirement.

These lessons convinced me of what, before that time, had been only an idea. To be a disciple, one is an evangelist, willing to share the personal story of the joy of forgiveness. One cannot follow Christ without being an evangelist. There is no option.

To be sure, discipleship, following Jesus Christ, and "evangelship," sharing one's story, are not synonymous. They are distinct. Discipleship means "followership"—movement, living by the fruits of the Spirit. When one lives deeds of kindness, gentleness, self-control, love, joy, peace, faithfulness, and patience, one is a disciple. But more is entailed for a full picture of the Christian life.

The other side of the coin completes the picture as one witnesses "in the name of Christ" and answers the inquiry "Why?" by sharing the joyous story of being forgiven. "Evangelship" is sharing the story of forgiveness, the joy of our salvation. Discipleship is living one's faith through deeds. "Evangelship" is sharing one's faith through words and witness. Discipleship and evangelship are as inseparable as justification and sanctification in the Pauline-Wesleyan view of Christian existence.

Evangelism and Church Growth

My experience with the church growth movement is that it often has nothing to do with the evangelistic task. Congregations and denominations can grow through a variety of means, including marketing strategies, which will attract previously committed Christians to transfer their memberships to that fellowship or congregation. These congregations and denominations may grow without one single soul experiencing, for the first time, the joy of forgiveness, or in more classical terms, being born again.

When I was in Africa, I discovered that church growth is not a goal there. The United Methodist Church is growing tremendously, but growth is not the goal. The goal is faithful witnessing for Christ. Human beings are responsible to be faithful witnesses. God determines if the human witness will lead to church growth. Faithful witnessing then is the goal.

This is an important lesson for The United Methodist Church. Our strategy for the evangelistic task has been to determine the demographic movement of "our kinds of people," buy a piece of property exposed to the highest traffic count, appoint a likeable person as pastor, build a building, open the doors at the most convenient time of the day, and be smart enough to get out of the way so we won't get trampled as people rush in. We call this church growth and believe it is the consequence of having church growth as a goal. However, often, the unchurched have not been reached. New persons affiliate with the church having had no personal experience of the joy and peace brought by forgiveness in Christ.

By contrast, in Angola, twenty years ago, a young pastor emerged from prison to be elected as the first indigenous bishop among the Angolan people. Bishop Emilio de Carvalho had no goal that the church would grow. His goal was to be a faithful witness. He traveled around the country simply being a faithful witness, telling God's stories in light of his own story. As a consequence of this faithful witness, others became faithful witnesses. The church has grown phenomenonally through reaching the unchurched.

The distinction is clear and radical. The goal of the church must be to become a faithful witness. Every United Methodist is to be an evangelist. We are unfaithful when we are not evangelists. As I read church history, the story of Africa today is consistent with God's actions for thousands of years. Faithful witnessing almost always leads to church growth; but whenever church growth replaces faithful witnessing as a goal, the church always declines. This is certainly true in The United Methodist Church. Decline cannot be turned around by the church deciding its goal is to grow. Decline can only be turned around by the church deciding to be a faithful witness.

I also discovered in Africa that church growth is measured by professions of faith, not membership growth. In Africa, membership growth is not church growth. God's arithmetic does not compute when a person of faith transfers from one congregation to another. God's computation occurs when one who was in darkness sees the light, when one who was in bondage is freed, when one who was born once is born again.

In Zimbabwe, I preached to a new congregation in a neighborhood where, prior to independence in 1980, an African could not live. It had previously been a segregated community. This congregation was meeting in a school building, and it was overflowing. That afternoon I visited with the laity of the congregation and observed that they were a remarkable example of church growth in Africa. I was quickly corrected. They shared with me that most of them were not new Christians, that they had simply gathered together existing persons of faith. They pointed out that church growth would only occur when persons became new Christians in their congregation. To them, mere membership growth did not mean that there had been church growth. I learned in Africa to understand God's arithmetic. This is why, since coming back from that country, I look in a new way at statistical reports. I now look for how many persons have joined by profession of faith, for this is truly church growth. I no longer look at the column of church membership.

These lessons have enabled me to understand that faithful witnessing always leads to church growth as persons experience, for the first time, the joy of forgiveness. However, membership growth often occurs without any indication of real evangelism. Authentic church growth occurs when the unchurched are reached or, in my own words, the unforgiven experience forgiveness and become part of the community of forgiven people.

The Context of Evangelism

Many forms and structures of and for the evangelistic task are based upon or operate within the context of judgment. This "ethos of judgment" is pervasive in planning, in training, and in the implementation of strategies related to the evangelistic task. Increasingly, I receive the same message from committed Christians and from persons who inquire about the faith. What they say is, "If being a Christian requires one to look, act and communicate in a disparaging or judgmental way toward the unchurched, the unfaithful, or persons of other faiths, then I reject the Christian faith." Informed Christians who hold this perspective base it upon their understanding of the New Testament, including the life and teachings of Jesus Christ. The oft-quoted text is "Do not judge, so that you may not be judged" (Matt. 7:1). In response, the resounding voices of others affirm that one must have a zeal for the Christian faith. This position is defended with the biblical message, "Believe on the Lord Jesus, and you will be saved" (Acts 16:31).

From time to time debate breaks forth in the church between those who hold to this view (which could be called a *conditional universalism*) and advocates of a more open universalism. Often the debate is heated. The theological issues here are crucially important because they focus upon our understanding of salvation. Because they focus upon the matter of salvation, we should exercise reserve before reaching negative judgments. Ultimately the working of saving grace exceeds the full grasp of our minds.

I reject the behavioral attitudes often accompanying this debate. This is not to plead theological indifference. Yet, I observe persons who are the most effective evangelists telling their stories with zeal! Period! They also are willing to allow others to tell their stories with zeal. They stop short of communicating in any way that their stories are better than those of others. Removed from the context of judgment, these persons are ambassadors, telling the credible story of being forgiven and living in a community of forgiven people. They leave the issue of salvation in the hands of God.[1]

As I observe these grace-filled evangelists, I see clearly the consequences of sharing the credible message of the good news of forgiveness. Persons who have not experienced personal forgiveness are drawn like a magnet to the liberating experience of being freed from the shackles of guilt and anxiety. Often, religious persons who have journeyed alone are attracted to a community of forgiven people as opposed to communities filled with guilt, anxiety, and what Paul called "works of the flesh: . . . fornication, impurity, licentiousness, idolatry, sorcery, enmities, strife, jealousy, anger, quarrels, dissensions, factions, envy, drunkenness, carousing, and things like these" (Gal. 5:19-21).

If the governors of one's life are guilt and anxiety, the prospect of forgiveness is compelling. If the communities of one's life are based on the deeds of the flesh, then the prospect of living within the community of forgiven people can be compared to coming upon an oasis in the desert. On the other hand, if the story of the Jesus the Evangelist is told in the context of judgment, the guilt and anxiety of one's life become more intense. If the community is one where deeds of the flesh dominate, there is no attraction, for it is as every other community. To be an evangelist of grace compels one to tell the story of good news, the joy of forgiveness, and mandates the church to be a community of forgiveness. To be an evangelist of grace is not easy, but the task is quite simple.

To be an evangelist of grace is to be faithful to our tradition as United Methodists. In 1988, the Study Commission on the Mission of the United Methodist Church reported its work to General Conference. It was entitled "Grace Upon Grace."[2] Why? Because that is the way the Methodist class meeting began in the cradle of the Church of England. That is the way the Methodists spread like wildfire on the prairie in the cradle of the American frontier. That is the distinctive characteristic of The United Methodist Church in the cradle of God's future as we anticipate the twenty-first century. "Grace Upon Grace!" On the foundation of grace, United Methodists live the faith. We are grace-filled evangelists.

Conclusion

In 1995, it is a waste of time to talk about the subject of the evangelistic task unless we first deal with the message. I am convinced many layers of the message are no longer credible. These layers include theological understandings which are the creation of the church, intended to assist in the interpretation and proclamation of the good news. The message of the Evangelist did not focus on these layers. The message of evangelists must not be these layers. The only credible message is the good news—"your sins are forgiven." This credible message was spoken by Jesus Christ in his ministry and from the cross. Only when we evangelists tell our story as disciples following the way the Evangelist lived and shared his story, will we be faithful disciples.

Furthermore, only as the church, the community of faith, lives its life as a community of forgiven persons who forgive one another, will the credible message be packaged in such a way that others will become a part of the community of faith. If the community is one of dissension, enmity, strife, jealousy, outbursts of anger, disputes, factions, and envy, the world will say as many have said, "If it were not for Christians, I could consider being a Christian." To assist in understanding the sources of these conclusions, I want to conclude with a short story.

From 1984 to 1988 the Oak Grove Church was abandoned. A few faithful continued to meet, unwilling to believe there was not a future for God's church in that location. In 1988, the district superintendent said "Why not?" and the ecclesiastical resurrection occurred. Numbers increased, involvement became meaningful, and pastoral leadership was appointed. Under this new leadership the Oak Grove congregation easily identified two rural communities it existed to serve. It wrestled with naming the third community. It was a rural trailer park next door to the church. The congregation finally said "yes" and named the trailer park in its statement of purpose.

After over a year of wrestling with what this meant, the church started a five-day-a-week after-school program in November, 1994. The members were excited as seven children began to attend. One week later twenty-two children were attending and still continue to attend. The people of Oak Grove Church were unabashedly evangelistic while being careful not to put the children or their parents down for not being active in church or faith.

Theresa professed her faith within a month. She came because the Oak Grove Church reached out to her children. She told me the week after she joined that others would come. When I preached there on December 4, 1994, there were twenty children in worship, two of whom were Theresa's children. One of the previously unchurched children said to me, "I prayed for you." The children were first in line for the potluck dinner. Adults in the church helped them fill their plates. A child asked me about a dish she had never seen before. I explained it to her and she said, "It will be as good as everything else at this church." When I asked her to continue, she looked at me and said, "They love me."

For many years the Oak Grove Church was, corporately, a "faithful disciple," receiving, primarily, transfers of membership. Only as the congregation has become evangelistic has it experienced authentic church growth. One remarkable commentary on our new society today is that, of the twenty-two children, only two of them knew that Christmas had anything to do with Jesus.

This story and many others have led me to these three discoveries about discipleship and the evangelistic task: (1) *discipleship and the evangelistic task are two sides of the same coin;* (2) *the evangelistic task and church growth are not the same,* and (3) *a distinctive mark of United Methodism is that the evangelistic task is fulfilled in the context of grace, not judgment.* I share these discoveries because they are both biblical and Wesleyan, and because they enable both the church and the message to be experienced as credible.

PART THREE

Frontiers

IN THE PRESENCE OF GOD and of Christ Jesus, who is to judge the living and the dead, and in view of his appearing and his kingdom, I solemnly urge you: proclaim the message; be persistent whether the time is favorable or unfavorable; convince, rebuke, and encourage, with the utmost patience in teaching. For the time is coming when people will not put up with sound doctrine, but having itching ears, they will accumulate for themselves teachers to suit their own desires, and will turn away from listening to the truth and wander away to myths. As for you, always be sober, endure suffering, do the work of an evangelist, carry out your ministry fully.

2 Timothy 4:1-5

THEN IT WAS SUNDAY MORNING, the birthday of God's gracious new age. There were no men to be found, yet, at that place where Jesus was laid to rest. True to the long account, women came first. Theirs it was to deliver the good news. God's chromosomes, "Xs" and "Ys," we call them, seem to make men such easy doubters. "Some women of our company have astounded us . . . they returned with a story . . . but him they did not see," so reports St. Luke. Aren't you thankful that the women went, saw, began to believe, and reported the Sunday mystery?

Bishop Edwin C. Boulton

CHAPTER 7

Multicultural Evangelism

Hae-Jong Kim

As WE REFLECT about evangelism, our clue is the Incarnation. *The Word became flesh and dwelt among us.* That, in essence, is the uniquely Christian gospel, Evangel *(euangelion)* which we proclaim. God's incarnation in Jesus Christ personally revealing eternal love to humankind is the good news. Sharing, spreading and proclaiming this evangel is called "evangelism." Therefore in this broader definition of evangelism, one can say, *evangelism is not a program or a task of the church, but rather the church is God's continuing program of evangelism.* After all, the church is, in a functional sense, the continuation of the Incarnation.

The Word Became Flesh and Dwelt Among Us

The Incarnation manifests not only the good news of God's act in creation, but also of God's love in redemption. The essence of the good news is that when we cannot reach God, God reaches out to us. When we cannot go over to God, God comes over to us. Such was the thesis of Nygren's classic study of "agape love."[1] John's epistle expresses it concisely:

> God's love was revealed among us in this way: God sent his only Son into the world so that we might live through him. In this is love, not that we loved God, but that he loved us and sent his Son to be the atoning sacrifice for our sins (1 John 4:9-10).

The Incarnation was a bridging event. Jesus Christ in his ministry, death, and resurrection was God's "suspension bridge" of love. One cannot find the word "bridge" in the Scriptures, but the concept of bridging is used from Genesis to Revelation. To come over, cross over, or go over means to bridge. In contemporary English, the prefix "trans-" carries that concept of bridging. In that sense, then, the Incarnation was the ultimate "trans-event."

The prefix "trans-" conveys the concept of bridge—going across or going beyond. The Incarnation is God's love transcending all other loves by becoming flesh and dwelling among us. God took the initiative and came into the world, into our lives, our history and our culture by "becoming flesh." *O logos sarx egeneto.* This "trans-event" was and is the good news. The Incarnation, this "trans-event," is the paradigm for multicultural evangelism. I will use three "trans-" words or concepts—translation, transmission, and transformation—in speaking of this critical dimension of evangelism.

Translation

The Word became flesh and dwelt among us to *translate* the mind of God, the *logos*, or the love of God, into our language and within our cultural context. Christ was born into a culture. He was born the son of Mary and Joseph, and grew up in Nazareth as a Jewish boy. He was fully a man of the first-century Jewish culture. That was how God intended to reveal the divine love to a beloved people at that time, within that cultural context. The divine Word was translated into the Hebrew culture. If we take the Incarnation as the paradigm of evangelism, then it follows that the gospel must be spoken in the language of the people. The gospel must take cultural thought forms that permit it to be grasped and understood. In short, as the Word took flesh, so must the gospel take cultural form.

Several years ago, I was doing a workshop on bilingual ministry for the National Asian Convocation. An African American brother introduced me by saying, "I understand that Dr. Kim speaks several languages. But me, I only speak two languages—English and ghettoese." Although said jokingly, his comment was a profound observation. In order to speak to the people in the street, one has to speak the language of the street. Translation then is the first order of incarnation.

A Personal Story of Translation

During the Korean War many American soldiers came to Korean soil and fought to free South Koreans from the aggressors. Among them an American Marine chaplain came full of zeal to share the gospel with the Korean people. He did not speak a word of Korean. I, a teenage refugee boy who spoke some English and was in desperate need of a job, met him and became his interpreter. I translated his message to Korean audiences, including a leper congregation we visited every Sunday for nine months. The word of God became flesh and dwelt among them through my translation. Through this experience more than one thousand people came to accept Christ in their lives and I, too, decided to give my life to Christ as a minister of the gospel. Evangelism was happening through linguistic and conceptual translation.

♦ ♦ ♦

Yes, the Incarnation is a "trans-lational event." God speaks to us in different accents and in different contexts. This is the message of the account of Pentecost in Acts 2. The language barriers were crossed. As Paul wrote, "Christ is our Peace, who has broken down the barriers between people." It is the very nature of incarnation that barriers are broken down or crossed so that the universality of the gospel becomes operative in the given context and moment.

The Incarnation in Jesus Christ happened with both *universality* and *particularity*. Paul refers to the particularity as the "scandal of the gospel." In fact the uniform witness of Scripture is that in this one, particular event, Jesus was *born*, within a *Jewish context*, and *"suffered under Pontius Pilate and was crucified."* At the same time, without denying the particularity, Scripture and the church witness to the universality of this event. The Kingdom which he proclaimed and which he incarnated was a universal reign of God. "They shall come," he said, "from the East and from the West."

As has always been the case, this universal Word in the particular form of Jesus Christ needs to be presented to the current age, within the current culture, through a language people understand, and through the idioms and mediums of particular cultures. This is why some of our ethnic communities require language churches, such as the Korean Church. In such a setting the gospel is inculturated.

A Second Personal Story of Translation

In the early 1970s, while I was a pastor in the Northern New Jersey Conference serving an English-speaking Caucasian congregation, the Korean immigrant population began to expand. The need for a Korean language worship service was evident. The people needed to hear the gospel in their native language and in their native thought forms. At first it was difficult to convince annual conference leaders, including the bishop, that we needed to provide "language ministries" to the Korean community. We needed to prove that there was a significant Korean population.

I devised what I later called the "Kim formula." The method was simple—look through the telephone directory and count the number of Kims listed. The Korean surname Kim makes up about twenty percent of the Korean population. Therefore, it follows, if you count all the Kims and multiply them by five, you will have the approximate size of the Korean community within that telephone directory area. I came up with twenty Kims, which translated into about one hundred families in the area. I sent out invitations to them, announcing that we were having a Korean language service. For the first service, fourteen people showed up including a family that had never been to church. It was the beginning of an exciting ministry.

Today, over twenty years later, there is a very strong Korean congregation with a Sunday attendance of four hundred. Today in that same telephone directory there are at least one thousand Kims. That means there are at least five thousand Korean families, most of whom will respond to a Korean language ministry. Today there are nine Korean United Methodist churches to meet the need and face the challenge. This growth and development has occurred since the first church was established in 1972. On the national scene, most Korean American congregations in the United States were established since 1970. Prior to that, there were only six. Today there are more than three hundred Korean United Methodist churches.

♦ ♦ ♦

Similar stories are repeated of other ethno-cultural groups, including many other Asian American communities. The Hispanic community has the same need and the National Hispanic Plan is our effort to evangelize that community through this incarnational paradigm of multicultural ministry.

An immigrant community lives in a dual cultural context—the American dominant culture and the ethnic culture. This duality of cultural contexts has to be taken seriously if we are serious about evangelism. The gospel must be translated into the language and thought forms of the various groups. Some ethnic groups do not have a visible community. They are blended into the majority community and become invisible. The fact is they live in two communities: the visible neighborhood community and the other invisible *ethno-urbia*, the ethnic cultural network which is visible only during special gatherings, such as services of worship.

For evangelism, the "English only" approach and mentality will not be effective. We need to take cross-cultural, incarnational ministry seriously. Today even in a Korean American church we see multicultural approaches. For second generation Koreans, English is their mother tongue and the American culture is their native culture. The same principle of *translation* applies here, but obviously the translation process is much more complex.

Transmission

Jesus Christ came to *transmit* the love of God. The Word became flesh and dwelt among us so that God could be touched, seen and heard. God was present under the conditions of human existence. Again the Johannine epistle explicitly affirms this:

> We declare to you what was from the beginning, what we have heard, what we have seen with our eyes, what we have looked at and touched with our hands, concerning the word of life. (1 John 1:1)

This means that evangelism as the *transmission* of the gospel is not only linguistic translation but convictional contagion as well. We have to "catch" it before we can give it to someone else. Today as a Christian people, are we too sanitized to transmit anything? George Hunter talks about this dimension of the paradigm in his book *The Contagious Congregation*.[2] Transmissive contagion cannot be encapsulated in an intellectual definition. It is personally convictional and communally generated.

Robert Wuthnow, in *Christianity in the Twenty-First Century*, writes about the need to transmit our identity as the Christian community if there is to be social continuity for the church.[3] Another sociologist with a group of colleagues writes of the church as a community of memory.[4] Contagion is simultaneously personal and communal.

John Wesley's message of prevenient, justifying, and sanctifying grace has been transmitted in many cultural ways and in many cultural settings. The identity of the Korean church is vivid witness to this. A dynamic message of experiential grace has over the generations become the identifying memory of the Korean church. The implicit universality of that message of grace has informed the Korean church making it a vital evangelistic and missionary church today. A monocultural church becomes a genuinely multicultural missionary movement.

The result of cross-cultural transmission is "disciples of all nations," baptized "in the name of the Father and of the Son and of the Holy Spirit" (Matt. 28:19), a people constantly being taught the commands of Christ and living in obedience to him. This was the vision which motivated Dr. Henry G. Appenzeller, the first Methodist missionary to Korea in 1885. He and his wife, a new bride, brought the gospel to the people of Korea, through their incarnational presence. Many other missionaries followed to transmit the Wesleyan spirit and ethos. Today there are at least 1.3 million Methodist Christians in Korea.

A Personal Story of Transmission

My family was converted during the Korean War while we were living as refugees, away from home. The gospel was transmitted to us by loving and hospitable hosts who shared their home (which could hardly be called a house by today's standards). The man was a class leader in the newly formed Methodist church. Through this contact and their gracious, but purposeful invitation, my mother first went to that small thirty-member church, met Christ, was converted, began attending class meetings, and grew in discipleship. As her faith began to mature, she had a vision for her four children. She began to pray for our future, though at that time our life was very tenuous and precarious at best. She prayed, every morning as she attended the early morning prayer meetings, "God, I am only a poor widow, a refugee, I don't have much to offer to you. I have four children. They are my offering. I commit them to you for I have no resource of power to take care of them. Take them and use them according to your will." Today all four of us and our spouses are in active ministry in The United Methodist Church.

The small group structure in the Korean church is an effective means of evangelistic outreach. The story of my mother is but one illustration of this. The late Donald McGavran has emphasized that the gospel travels best through familiar and already established social networks.[5] Certainly, the Korean church experience is evidence of contagious growth through small groups such as prayer groups and Wesleyan class meetings. Wuthnow challenges us: "Should congregations as we now know, be replaced by the shopping mall and the television?" The transmission of the gospel occurs most effectively through the incarnate structures of the local church, that is, through small groups such as Wesleyan classes.

Transformation

The purpose of the "trans-event" of Incarnation was transformation. The Word became flesh and dwelt among us and brought conversion. Our ministry, the incarnational ministry of the church, is to bring transformation through conversion in human life, individuals, societal structures, values, and systems. Somehow we have become afraid to use the word "conversion" because certain groups of people have been wrongly monopolizing it. Conversion, however, is a central aspect of Christian experience. It simply means "to change, "to be transformed."

Transformation works in various ways. On the one hand, one can experience a life-changing religious transformation. On the other hand, one can experience a gradual process of cultural conversion and transformation. The latter is often present in the contemporary church. The pressure and the power of the culture have been so great for many that the dominant culture has infiltrated our churches and transformed us.

We should heed the warning of people like George Barna, who reminds us that the church today has become like a frog in a kettle. You know the fable of the frog who allowed itself to be cooked in the kettle? Had the water been hot to begin with, the frog would have jumped out quickly. But, because the water was at first lukewarm and comfortable, and then gradually heated, the frog remained in the kettle. Therefore, the frog, without its knowledge, was being cooked. The church has been cooked by the secular culture because the temperature has been rising ever so gradually and comfortably.

To confront such a situation, Stanley Hauerwas and William Willimon tell us that in our increasingly secularized culture a new paradigm is needed for the church, namely, a "colony" "against the world for the world."[6] We can no longer survive, argues Willimon, within the chapel syndrome. We need to believe once again in the power of the gospel and the power of God to transform. In a similar way Loren Mead writes of the situation today which confronts the church if it would dare to be missionary. The contemporary church, to use Mead's analysis, is in a post-Christendom time. The paradigm of Christendom no longer prevails. In many respects the church is situated in a paradigm setting similar to what Mead calls "the apostolic paradigm."[7]

In the Acts of the Apostles, a miraculous transformation takes place. From the Incarnation in the person of Jesus and through the work of the Holy Spirit, the band of disciples is transformed to be the missionary Body of Christ, to translate and to transmit the gospel and thereby to transform the world. Certainly the day of Pentecost was a multicultural and a transcultural experience. The apostles, empowered by the Holy Spirit, spoke in the languages and dialects of the people crowding the Jerusalem streets (Acts 2). But this was only the beginning—the beginning of the transformation of the disciples to be the missionary church.

In subsequent chapters of Acts, we read about multicultural evangelism in its original and fundamental forms. Saul became Paul, transformed to preach the gospel of transformation. New congregations are established and become transformational congregations within their cultural contexts. The Pentecost experience repeats itself. In some dramatic way the Holy Spirit confirms the crossing of the various cultural frontiers. The Jerusalem church sends Peter and John to Samaria, thereby crossing the frontier of national boundaries, "and they received the Holy Spirit" (Acts 8:17). Philip, on the way from Jerusalem unto Gaza, encounters the unnamed man of Ethiopia, interprets the Scriptures to him, and baptizes him, and then "the Spirit of the Lord snatched Philip away" (Acts 8:39). The frontier of race had been crossed! When Peter responded to the call of God to meet and enter into hospitality with the Centurion, Cornelius, the frontier of cultic legalism was crossed (Acts 12:1f.). It was, indeed, a multicultural message which Peter preached: "God is no respecter of persons."

Our world may very well be post-Christendom. The church's cultural context may very well be similar to the church in the apostolic age. To be a missionary church in such a time will require the contemporary church to renew a sense of apostolic confidence. Leander Keck has recently pointed out that we have turned in the interpretation of Scripture from a *hermeneutics of suspicion* to a *herme-*

neutic of alienation. We have become an alienated people. Keck suggests that we should move from the *hermeneutics of suspicion* to a *hermeneutics of affirmation,* believing the power of the Word of God is still able to effect change and transformation. Only then can the church be "the church confident."[8]

A Personal Story of Transformation

In this regard, I want to share my favorite story of conversion, which is my grandfather's story: his conversion took place over a period of years, indeed, in a missionary situation.

When my family came back after two years of a long and hard refugee life, we returned as Christians. When we left Seoul on that cold winter day in January 1951, we were sure we would return to Seoul within a week or two. But our refugee life lasted for two years. During those years, God was gracious to us and we found Christ, and through Christ, we found God.

When we returned, my mother's father lived with us in our home for part of the year. He was unhappy that we were Christians because he practiced the teachings of Confucius. He was a scholar of Confucius. Christian people don't practice ancestor worship as taught by the tradition of Confucius. The fact that we were now a Christian family threatened that practice of ancestor worship, so he was unhappy.

During the two or three months in which he stayed with us every year, we had him attend our morning family devotions. I lost my father during the Korean War. Therefore, I was acting, although only a teenager, as head of the household and led the worship most of the time. My grandfather was almost forced to sit and worship with us; after all, we lived in a one-room house. There was no other place to go. From time to time I would try to preach to him, to influence him, but that didn't work very well.

One day, we urged him to go to church with us, and he did. After the service, he voiced a good impression of the church. He was touching his long beard and said: "Ah, hem ... ah hem. That wasn't too bad." We were so happy. We knew this was a good start.

We kept up our effort. The following year when we took him to church, the pastor presented him with a Bible. The pastor was a man of wisdom. He did not give him a Korean Bible but a Chinese Bible. He knew that my grandfather had knowledge of the Chinese language as a scholar in Confucius' teachings. My grandfather was so happy to receive this Bible, because he knew that his language knowledge was being recognized by this young pastor. He began to read the Gospels as we instructed him. He was shaking his head back and forth, even though the Bible was written vertically. He could not believe the things he was reading. He couldn't believe that Jesus fed five thousand people with five loaves of bread. He said, "This is incredible. I cannot believe it."

The following year when he returned to be with us again, he brought his Bible. God gave me the wisdom to say, "Grandpa, don't read the Gospels anymore, because these are too difficult for you. But try instead Proverbs." He opened Proverbs and began to read and said, "Aha! Here is some truth." He liked Proverbs and he began to enjoy reading the Bible, because like the teachings of Confucius, the collection of Proverbs is Wisdom literature. He continued to enjoy reading Proverbs. The following year he returned with his Bible, and told us that he had read Proverbs many times and had enjoyed it. Now he was reading Ecclesiastes! He was coming into the Christian faith through Wisdom literature—a back door, so to speak.

The process of the conversion of my grandfather took over five years. The fifth year, when he was eighty-five, we were sitting together in devotional worship again, and singing a hymn about Jesus lifting our burdens. After the hymn he was moved and said, "Let us sing again. It is a good hymn." So we sang the hymn again with gusto. After the hymn, he said, "I have been thinking. I want to be baptized." We took him to our pastor, who gave him instruction. My grandfather memorized the Ten Commandments and the Lord's Prayer and the Apostles' Creed. Kneeling before this young pastor, my grandfather was baptized. A transformation took place in his heart and life.

While my grandfather was being baptized in the name of the Father, and the Son, and the Holy Spirit, he suddenly prayed aloud a simple prayer. "Oh God, we thank you for saving me, such a sinner." He lived for another year as a Christian. When he died, the young pastor was beside him. Conscious up to the very end of his life, my grandfather knew he was dying, but in faith in Jesus Christ. He had been transformed by the power of the Word of God.

♦ ♦ ♦

So we are the "trans-agents," the continuing incarnation of Jesus Christ, bringing the translation, the transmission, and the transformation of the gospel to all cultures. The church of Jesus Christ is not a corporation or a business organization, but rather the *corpus Christi*, the missionary body of Christ. A new paradigm is called for to bring the gospel into the cultural expressions of various people through translation; to transmit the love of God through our contacts as a contagious congregation; and to bring the news of transformation in and through Christ into a world of hopelessness, conflict, and fear.

The ultimate challenge of this paradigm of Incarnation is the theology of *kenosis*, Christ emptying himself in flesh, becoming a servant, obedient unto death, even death on the cross. In this servant form, the transformed body of Christ is an inclusive entity—one body with diverse members, unity within diversity, a multicultural, multiracial, multiethnic, multiclass, multigenerational community. Evangelism means that we become trans-agents, to translate and transmit the gospel that brings transformation to the world.

CHAPTER 8

Multicultural Evangelism: A Response from a Hispanic American Perspective

Elias G. Galvan

WHEN I SPEAK about the evangelistic task of our church among Hispanics, I do not mean United Methodist Hispanic churches reaching Hispanic people. The National Plan for Hispanic Ministries, approved by the General Conference of 1992, is clear that reaching the Hispanic community is the task of the entire church. It is important to keep this in mind because our church is predominantly Euro-American and English-speaking in a society that is becoming increasingly multicultural and multilingual. Papers like the one presented by Bishop Kim are of great importance for the mission of our church into the future. If we are serious in presenting the gospel of Christ to people of Hispanic ancestry, then we must prepare ourselves and discover fresh and effective ways to reach them. The Hispanic community in our country is growing at a very fast rate. By the year 2010, the U.S. census is predicting that this minority will become the largest ethnic minority in this country, surpassing the 45,000,000 mark. If we are to reach them with the ministry of our church, *every* local church located in areas where Hispanics live must find ways to reach out and intentionally include them in our evangelistic outreach.

It is not a secret that we as a denomination, in spite of our interest and success in areas like Texas and New Mexico, have not made substantial inroads into this culture. There are areas in our country where, even though the Hispanic community is growing rapidly, Hispanic churches are decreasing in size. Hispanics are not increasing in our English-speaking congregations, and ministries that in past years served them are now being reduced or closed.

Bishop Kim is theologically correct in stating that the foundation of multicultural evangelism is the doctrine of the Incarnation. For me, it is impossible to begin anywhere else in my own understanding of evangelism. There is no evangelism without incarnation. The good news of the gospel is, as the apostle reminds us, the fact that "in Christ God was reconciling the world unto himself" (2 Cor. 5:19). The evangelistic task assumes that God addresses persons in Jesus Christ in the moment in which they live and in the situation in which they find themselves. Therefore, as Bishop Kim points out, *translation* becomes a very important concept when we speak about multicultural evangelism. Translation is not just the transliteration of words from one language to another, but it implies entering into another culture, making real the love of God in the context where persons live. Incarnation as translation implies a close identification with the other to whom we are to witness. Orlando Costas refers to this kind of witness as "contextual evangelization":

> An evangelistic witness is a person who is not ashamed to let everyone see and hear about his or her experience of God, who identifies with and appropriates the fears and hopes of others, and who from that vantage point shares lovingly, even passionately, the gospel in word and deed. . . . [Such witness] takes place in a given social and historical context.[1]

Missionaries traveling to other countries try, with varying degrees of success, to enter into the culture of the people with whom they seek to minister. Here in the U.S., however, the problem of translation has become rather complicated for several reasons. First, the assumption has been that "language churches" are temporary and transitional. Second, the Protestant church has historically seen itself as a channel for assimilation of Hispanics into the larger society. Third, there has been little interest in understanding and preserving the Hispanic culture. Hispanic culture has often been perceived as inferior or at least unnecessary for the new immigrants to function adequately in our country. Previous attempts to evangelize this minority have used the same methods of evangelism used in the majority culture with limited success.

Again, Orlando Costas reminds us that

evangelization is first and foremost a human encounter.... The first thing one shares in any evangelistic situation is oneself with one's human limitation. One never evangelizes as an angel or a better-than-thou heavenly creature.[2]

In the past, when Spanish has been used in our evangelism, we have failed to understand the cultural context of the people we have tried to reach. Evangelism among Hispanics has to be personal, relational, and contextual. It has to be done from a position of equality. If we are to reach the Hispanics, they need to see in us persons "who share the same precarious existence ... and who are part of the same world of sinners and victims of sin."[30]

One of the most effective tools to reach Hispanics is hospitality. Hospitality as a tool for evangelism is not a new concept. Several have spoken and written about this type of evangelism. It has been used effectively by those who have engaged in interreligious dialogues, among them the great evangelist E. Stanley Jones.[4] Hospitality is a biblical concept whose importance must be recovered today.[5] In the words of Henri Nouwen,

> Hospitality is one of the richest biblical terms that can deepen and broaden our insight in our relationships to our fellow human beings. Old and New Testament stories not only show how serious our obligation is to welcome the stranger in our home, but they also tell us that guests are carrying precious gifts with them.[6]

Hospitality is more than inviting someone into our home. It is a matter of attitude toward other human beings. Hospitality implies a willingness to receive the other as a child of God, to receive him or her with the respect and dignity accorded to someone created in God's image. Hospitality is creating the space where true dialogue takes place, a dialogue where we share and receive, teach and learn, a place where authentic witness takes place. It is not a place where we push a person into a corner where no alternative is left, but rather it is the space where a person, without feeling intimidated, manipulated, or coerced, hears God's voice and chooses to make a commitment to follow Christ. Hospitality acknowledges God's prevenient grace working in the guest as well as in the host.

G. Howard Mellor, writing on evangelism and religious pluralism, speaks about the importance of the doctrine of incarnation in evangelism with its insistence that the gospel is about a "With-Us-

God."[7] Therefore, in the sharing of the good news, we need to embody in our own lives the message that we preach.

When we speak about reaching the ethnic minorities, especially the recent immigrants, hospitality becomes a crucial and indispensable tool. The implementation of this concept is particularly difficult for us because our society is becoming increasingly less hospitable. One of the trends many sociologists and futurists predict is what is called "cocooning." Persons are retreating to the safety of their homes and becoming very selective about who is included in their inner circle. Faith Popcorn calls this trend "hyper-nesting."[8] Leonard Sweet refers to it as "the cave syndrome."[9] But there is another trend which is far more damaging to our evangelizing among ethnic minorities: the growing hostility toward those who are different.

A clear sign of such hostility is the xenophobia which is moving through our country. Proposition 187 in California is an indication of how deep these feelings are. Similar propositions are now being considered in many parts of the country. Several proposals that have been discussed in Congress would deprive even legal residents of access to any benefits; those proposals are part of this general mood. This movement has serious implications for our outreach among Hispanics. Members of the Hispanic community, even those born in the U.S., have interpreted this movement as anti-Hispanic. The level of trust between the majority and some ethnic minority groups is at its lowest ebb in many years. Similar hostile feelings are now being expressed openly within our church. Hostility leads to scapegoating, and regrettably, it is the marginalized, the powerless, those who are different, who are more often singled out as the scapegoat. It is in this milieu that the church must present the gospel of the reconciling love of God, but we will not be able to accomplish this unless we are able to turn hostility into hospitality. Hispanics need to see and experience a different attitude from the church. The practice of hospitality is indeed an indispensable factor in our evangelism among Hispanics.

Another reason why the emphasis on hospitality is important to our evangelism is that Hispanic people are very hospitable. Hospitality is a central element of Hispanic culture. Much time is spent in receiving and giving hospitality. Such practices are not limited only to the extended family but are open to friends and acquaintances. Even some of the monolingual people understand the hospitable greeting or invitation of *"mi casa es su casa."* Hospitality is something

Hispanics understand and will respond to if someone offers it to them.

Hispanic people, for the most part, will not respond to invitations to attend worship services or meetings that take place in Protestant churches. Their strong anti-Protestant upbringing prevents them from entering a Protestant sanctuary, but they will respond to an invitation to a home even if the invitation is to a Bible study group. The National Plan for Hispanic Ministries takes hospitality as a basic tool for evangelism. This is the case not only because Hispanics are accustomed to receiving and offering hospitality, but because Hispanics have extensive networks that they have developed through their practice of hospitality opening a wide possibility for evangelism.

Why is evangelism among Hispanics important? Because many are not being reached by the ministry of the church, any church. Most Protestants believe that all Hispanics are Catholic, and they assume that the Roman Catholic church is providing for their spiritual needs. Though the figures vary according to who quotes them, the sad reality is that only a small percentage are attending the Catholic church with any regularity and an even smaller percentage are affiliated with the Protestant churches, including the Pentecostals. One thing is clear, the Hispanics have the dubious distinction of being the most unchurched minority in the United States. This is the fact which causes me great concern.

Bishop Kim wisely points to the purpose of evangelism as the transformation of persons, societies, and the entire world. But he also adds, "The pressure and the power of the culture has been so great for many that it has infiltrated our churches." It is no surprise to discover that the same fears, feelings of alienation, frustration, and distrust that exist in society also are found in the church. After all, the church is part of society. What makes our evangelistic task more difficult is that these feelings have found a resounding echo in some of our members. It is difficult to speak an authentic word of God's love to those outside our church when we openly attack each other. It is difficult to speak about reconciliation with God when there is a "meanness" in our social and political relations. It is difficult to speak about transformation when we are not even open to honest dialogue with other members of the United Methodist family.

A Hispanic voice addressing The United Methodist Church, Bishop Mortimer Arias, points out that the task of evangelization has a double edge. He refers to centrifugal and centripetal evangelization.[10] When speaking of centripetal evangelization we must see our local congregations as fields of evangelization because, as Bishop Kim has pointed out, the church and the political ethos are often indistinguishable.

CHAPTER 9

Evangelism and Secularization

Ruediger R. Minor

A SOVIET PARABLE: Two "Kolkhozniki," farmers on a Soviet collective farm, look over the fields that are ripe for harvest. "Praise God for the good weather," one of them says, "we will have a record harvest." "But, comrade, don't you know that there is no God?" The other replies, "Yes, of course, but if—God forbid—there was a God?"[1]

To take the world *etsi deus non daretur*, "as if there was no God," is one of the principles foundational in the development of the modern scientific world view. This working hypothesis was changed to become a statement, "There is no God." The process of this change is *secularization*, its result *secularism*. There was no place in the world where this creed was so fiercely believed than in the official ideology of the Communist world. "There is no God, and Karl Marx is his prophet." And there was no other place where it became so obvious that secularism in fighting religion became a kind of religion itself.

Secularization—A Brief Definition

In what follows, the treatment of secularization is from a perspective of personal experience, a life at the edge of the political East and West for the second half of this century, first in East Germany and now in Russia. Some parts of this experience are probably very close to the experience of people in the (political and cultural) West, others are clearly different.

Looking for a short description of a "secular" world, we can begin with an examination of Harvey Cox's book of the mid-1960s, *The Secular City*,[2] one of the "holy texts" interpreting twentieth-century secularization. According to the title of the German translation (*Stadt ohne Gott*) the secular world is a "world without God." However, we will use this just as a phenomenological description, not a theological definition. It describes a process of diminishing influence of the church, its teaching religious norms, ethics, and behavior. This is understood as a process of liberation beginning in the time of the Enlightenment, the "exodus out of the status of minority" (Immanuel Kant).[3] It is accompanied by a growing self-awareness and autonomy of the human species.

Two important features of this process need to be mentioned. First, secularization has its historical, cultural, and geographic place in "Christendom," the so-called *Corpus Christianum*, which was (ideally) a system of theological, scientific, social, and political unity led by the medieval Christian ideal.

In the introduction to his book, *How to Reach Secular People*,[4] George Hunter gives a vivid description of the typical "Christian" person in the High Middle Ages and a modern "secular" person. The former lived in a society where one turned to the church for answers to all the questions of life: meaning, explanation, direction, authority. The posture was always one of the church in a pivotal, privileged position in society granting authorization for all kinds of activities.

The church was in a unique position; her "influence bordered on monopoly."[5] The secular person does not even know about the church as a source of orientation. He/she has a feeling of superiority over the ancestors, a freedom in decision-making; the world has "come of age" (Dietrich Bonhoeffer).[6] This is not the place to discuss how many weak points are in this position. Hunter's attitude, however, seems to give a negative mark to this development from the very beginning. In what I call a "Catholic" view, he sees enlightenment as the adversary to Christianity. We should remember, however, that among the first who sought freedom from a dominating church were the continental reformers, the English free church movement, and "evangelicalism" in its early forms of Pietism and Methodism. They contributed to the dissolution of a formal, established, dominating religion.

In this presentation we can only touch on the question whether there has been secularization in non-Christian cultures (especially in the East). Doubtless there are phenomena that resemble processes in the Western world. They could, however, be identified as byproducts of the Western influence (colonialism, imperialism, technological revolution).

Second, the process of secularization is to an important degree a legitimate continuation of the transformation of the world initiated by the influence of the Christian gospel. There would be no secularization without the idea of the world distinct from the deity. This is the revolutionary concept of Biblical teaching about creation. In the pagan religions the world was either of divine substance or of divine "waste." It was always under a religious spell. Biblical faith declares the world to be the dominion of human beings (Gen. 1:28), enabling the scientific and technological development of the West that is a result of the demythologization of the world. It was more than anti-Christian propaganda when the first Christians were declared "atheists" by the Roman authorities in state and religion.[7] The Christian faith was attacking a religious world view, and not defending it. This was true even as the church reestablished a religious world in "Christendom" after coming to power at the end of the Roman Empire.

The United States had no direct experience of this phase. A quotation from a German Baptist theological dictionary, however, gives an interesting evaluation of the process of secularization from a truly evangelical point of view:

> In the first instance the church indeed has liberated the world from the domination of pagan-sacred powers, but it yielded to the temptation to establish a sacred domination over the world in the Middle Ages. However, perceptions originating from the proclamation of the gospel resulted in protest and refusal against a development to take up a new, even Christian, yoke of slavery in the form of Christendom and a state church.[8]

Evangelism and proclamation of the gospel can accurately be equated in this statement. This means that evangelism should not be seen as a "remedy" against secularization in order to turn secularization back, but as a contributor to a legitimate secularization that opened the door for freedom of conscience and faith as well as science and technology.

Results of the Process of Secularization

After what has been said, there will be no surprise that, although I am not discussing their positions in detail, I agree with some German Protestant theologians (Bonhoeffer and Gogarten) who were seeking a positive theological assessment of this development.[9] Nowadays we find a regressive, conservative mood that denounces the liberation process from its very beginnings. It is especially strong under Roman and Orthodox auspices, and runs parallel to the attempt to nullify the modern world under the influence of a fundamentalist violent remaking of non-Christian cultures. We need to emphasize the legitimate use of the dominion conferred upon human beings against such attitudes. Despite all romanticism and frustrated criticism of modern culture, most of these people would not really like to live under the circumstances they idealize. The disenchantment with the first wave of conservative ruling in some of the Eastern European countries is but one proof of this. Hans Christian Andersen, in his fairy tale, "The Galoshes of Happiness," derides in a fine way the dreams of a turned-back idealizing of history. On the other hand, we dare not fail to see that the process of secularization is accompanied by a perversion of the divine commission given to human beings. A few examples from my experience in Russia and Eastern Europe will illustrate this.

(1) *The dominion has been turned to domination.* The imperative "have dominion" has been changed to almost arbitrary domineering. Soviet history is doomed with huge projects to change the face of the earth. Mountains have been removed; whole areas have been turned into large dam and canal projects. The Volga River is now a chain of huge artificial lakes; the inland seas of the Caspian Sea and the Aral Sea changed their character, the latter becoming almost extinct. There was even a project to stop the great Siberian rivers in mid-course and turn them back to the South to water the Kasakh steepe. I remember well from my time in school that we had to learn about all of these programs under the headline "Man, Master of Nature." There is no doubt that everywhere in the world nature has been treated in such a way. Nowhere, however, had such an extraordinary ideological interpretation and use of nature occurred as was seen in the Communist world. This ideological use and misuse of the natural world, both in theoretical and practical expressions, amounts to a human domination without limitation, a secular ideology.

(2) *Humankind has become the supreme being.* Again, we should not overlook the fact that here there is a certain similarity to the biblical message, the Psalmist sang:

> Thou hast made him little less than God. . . . Thou hast given him dominion. . . ; thou hast put all things under his feet. (Ps. 8:4-6, RSV)

It is biblical to speak of humans as supreme beings *under God.* Karl

Marx, however, set aside this restriction declaring that "man was supreme being for man." The result was that humans treated each other as lesser beings, sacrificing millions for the purity of an ideology, for gigantic goals, or for sheer lust of power and hatred. In denying the superiority of God, human beings became their own supreme law. What started as a process of liberation from outside authorities finally ended in a narcissistic, self-serving attitude. Again, this happened everywhere in the (former) "Christian world," but it was the Communist system that was spelling it out most clearly.

(3) *In fighting religion, secularism became a religion itself.* Religion, the Christian faith, was understood as the stronghold of the humiliating forces, and therefore everywhere the process of secularization included a phase of fighting against religion or at least some of its aspects or manifestations. Nowhere was religion as persecuted as in the Soviet Union; on the other hand, the secular ideology was so apparently expressed in religious forms. It is an open question (even among the "Sovietologists") whether the Soviet society was a secular one. If we talk of a secular society in the former Soviet Union we need to ask what kind of secularism it was. Soviet society was, I believe, a secular society that bore the face of a "secular religion." To a large degree Communism in the Soviet Union was acting like a religion. For example, the Communists destroyed the church buildings, but in order to build their party headquarters at the same places. Something very interesting is happening in Moscow right now. The largest church building in all of Orthodoxy, the Church of Christ Our Savior, had been destroyed in the thirties. There were plans to build in its place an immense central building for the Communists. Because of technical problems this plan never materialized. In its place a swimming pool was finally built. Now construction is under way to rebuild this church. I see this as an attempt to roll back Communist history. From the history of religions we know about the importance of the "holy places." For example, after the victory of the Christian church under Constantine, churches were built in ancient Rome at the very former places of the pagan temples. Another example, the cult of the Cosmonauts, could well be understood as a surrogate for the lost dimension of transcendence. Hardly a village exists in Russia where there is not a statue of Yuri Gagarin, the first Russian cosmonaut. The cult of the leaders and their pictures clearly resembles the icons and their role in the Eastern church. The religious forms were borrowed for a persuasion totally concerned with this world. The

basic trends were secular. Therefore, one can speak of a "secular religion."

It can fairly be stated that secularism has betrayed the liberating process that was connected to true secularization, turning the dominion over the earth into a new dependency on powers that could not be controlled, the liberation of humankind into a new slavery, and the freedom from the religious spell into a search party for all kinds of new and old cults.

Evangelizing the Secular Society

While evangelism should not be understood as an absolute "anti" to secularization, more and more a growing consensus is forming that views the secularized world as the field of evangelism. Even among more conservative evangelicals in countries with a strong national church/religious tradition, we recognize a positive attitude toward a "situation, that by its thorough secularization could clearly be recognized as a mission situation."[10]

(1) *There are strong forces now that try to win back the secularized world for some kind of renewed Christendom.* Pope John Paul II even calls this a "re-evangelization" of the world. Tendencies in Russia and the strong conservative wing of the Russian Orthodox Church follow the same direction. There is a tendency (again especially strong in Russia) to look at the "demolishing" of a Christian society as a process of the seven decades between 1917 and 1989. It is true, however, that the estrangement from religious forms had begun much earlier (even in Russia). The secular character of the Communist society was even more obvious in those Communist countries having a Western tradition, especially Czechoslovakia and East Germany. Professor Jukub Trojan, a Protestant theologian from Prague, observed recently that human beings in these countries had already given up Christian traditions a long time before they came under the influence of the "degraded Marxism of the Real Socialism."[11]

It is futile to think of a reestablishment of Christian traditions in the society. Trojan states that the Roman Catholic Church dreams of the possibility of leading the Czech area and even the whole of Europe back to the roots of the Christian tradition, but that it is not ready to see evangelization as a part of its own renewal. It hopes simply for a return to the positions before the Communists took power. What is said here about the Roman Catholic Church is *mutatis mutandis* also true for the Russian Orthodox Church, for which the concept of a reevangelization would include the affirmation of the medieval system of Christendom, the ruling of the world by ecclesiastical forces. Although we might express a deep understanding and admiration for this attempt to express the lordship of God over the world, we cannot condone the theory and practice of how the world was once "subjugated" under this lordship. Finally, it was not the lordship of God and Christ but of the "kings of the Gentiles" (Luke 22:25) who shaped this rulership, beginning with the Roman emperor Constantine.

(2) *The attempt to render a positive assessment of secularization should not lead to the temptation of using single moments of this process as a "point of contact."* From its history, evangelism has a tendency to make positive use, even to reinforce the individualism of the secular society. We should not be content with "reaching secular people." Evangelism is indeed directed toward the whole culture. A more contemporary temptation for evangelism is actually linked with a special feature of secular culture, the consumerist attitude to look for things that are pleasing to a person's desires and taste and to create those desires by marketing measures. Many modern evangelists fall prey to marketing ideas. Some of the modern handbooks for church growth even seem to be no more than marketing rules. Again, Russia in its struggle to build up a market economy is a very interesting test case even for religious marketing. Russia has recently been described as a "religious supermarket." Through the last four years the religious scene in Russia has incredibly changed. There are many new Christian groups that came from abroad. Most of them are conservative evangelicals. But there are also groups that represent Eastern spirituality and new cults. In the usual enumerations "Satanists" and "Krishnaites" are never left out. The whole neo-religious movement of the last three decades that has been kept out so carefully by the KGB is now suddenly present in Russia.

Most of these Christian groups come with good intentions but they have little or no knowledge about Russian history and spirituality. They come in an attitude of bringing Christ to the empire of evil. Many of them are self-centered and in doing evangelism they are serving their own cause. "They do not evangelize, they franchise." They come with high pretensions about their role and results. Although the reports over here about their numbers of churches and converts may sound impressive, this is not met by the reality in

Russia. Those reports are mostly intended to keep the financial resources flowing.

The new religious fundamentalism, the wave of occultism and irrationalism seems to contradict the idea of a secularist humanity. It might, however, be the companion of it. Secularism has not been without religion, although it said farewell to its dominant Christian expressions. The question therefore is, What kind of religion? John Wesley's use of the terms "true" and "false religion" might be helpful here. (We find this idea already with the Swiss reformer Ulrich Zwingli's *Commentary on True and False Religion*[12]). It is important to fill these terms with new meaning. For Zwingli true and false religion described the contradiction of Protestantism and Roman Catholicism. Wesley distinguished between "experimental," personal faith and "formal" religion. Today we could define "true religion" as serving individuals and society and "false religion" as just another consumer product to make persons feel good. The religious supermarket, the "religious shopping mall," is no sign that religion has finally overcome secularism. It is just the opposite: religion has been conformed to the secular market society.

(3) *The true meaning of evangelism in a secular society is to be found in a new interpretation of the lordship of God over the world.* Eberhard Jüngel, in an essay entitled "Secularization—Theological Notes to the Idea of a Secular World,"[13] states that "God reveals himself as the Lord of the world, however at the same time he shows himself as friend of man and his world." Jüngel quotes from a sermon of Martin Luther:

> The word Lord sounds friendly beyond measure here, it is a lovely and comforting word, . . . because he [God] has done this all and has wrought for us so much to save us, not that he would be a Lord who deals with us as a tyrant, compelling, punishing and terrifying us, but that we had a friendly, helpful lordship under which we could be safe and free of all violence and affliction.[14]

Authentic evangelism never leads back into a "yoke of slavery" (Gal. 5:1). And the evangelist is not the master but a servant of this servant Lord and of people (2 Cor. 4:5). A number of implications can be drawn for the contemporary practice of evangelism, again taking Russia as an example.

First, there is no realism in the dream of turning the clock back. This would be no guarantee for a more human world. Would we really hope for forms of clericalism and caesaro-papism in the future?

Second, the world will not become the "ward" of the church again—not even in Russia. The time is over for a dominating church. Even in the case that some conservative movements would take hold of power in Russia and grant the Russian Orthodox Church great privileges, it would not be a favor for the church. The church would soon realize that it became the victim and servant of the powerful.

Third, what are the chances for the church in a secular society such as Russia today? The task should not be to turn the society into a new "Christendom," into a new church-led body, but to assist it in being a human and humanizing society. If we believe that to be a Christian is to become more human in a deeper sense, then the churches should have an enabling influence in the world. In the present situation in Russia where people feel that the fundaments have been shaken, there is very much interest in new orientations and new directions, and the church can enable dialogues in offering such orientation.

(4) *Evangelism in a secular society must be done in dialogue.* G. Howard Mellor has reminded us of the New Testament use of the word "dialogizomai" as "argue-reason-content."[15] The evangelist is not the one who comes in a position of superiority or in the possession of the truth. Tactfulness and respect are his/her virtues. This includes taking the "vis-à-vis" seriously, sometimes more than he/she would do him/herself.[16]

In Russia there is a tendency to do away with the past and its principles that should not be exploited. We should not allow bribing people to become Christian believers, nor should we at the same time make them feel guilty that they were once honest atheists. Rather we should enable persons to explore the Christian faith by listening to the sharing, by studying the Bible, by experiencing a personal encounter with Christ. Otherwise, we would make the faith into a generic set of convictions and values, which would perfectly match John Wesley's description of "formal religion," be it Christian or secular.

(5) *Evangelism as the proclamation of the servant-lordship of the liberating Jesus Christ will defend the secular society and groups within this society against the imposition of a tradition that the secular society has rightfully done away with.* One of those areas secular society has rightfully done away with is the role and place of women in society. I am convinced that genuine evangelism in Russia is bringing a substantial contribution of the role of women. I only notice some

observations; however, I am careful not to draw far-reaching conclusions or to develop theories. Women are not only the majority in Russian churches (as everywhere), they have also (so far) in Russian Methodism the majority in leadership positions. This does not reflect the role of women in the Russian society, which is very patriarchal. The noted equal rights of women in the former Soviet Union existed more or less on paper only. Women were entitled to work as much and as hard as men did, and to care for family and households beside. It is interesting that they themselves comment on this with a certain pride about the strength of "Russian women." There is no doubt that women presently are paying the major price of societal changes. What does it mean that women occupy a distinguished role in the church? Would it finally be only a surrogate for their diminished role in society, or even only a new version of the ghettoizing of women with children, church, and kitchen (the well-known three "Ks" in German)? Or, would it be the sign of a real "evangelistic" liberation of women, which would of course only be possible if it would lead to a liberation of men as well?

(6) *Evangelism in a secular society is building a new church not as an end in itself but as a model for a servant community.* There is no need to add more pages to the often-told stories of restoration in the Russian Orthodox Church. Unfortunately, large circles understand church renewal as repair of buildings, reclaiming of political positions, and reintroduction of worship styles of the nineteenth century. This, however, is not the whole picture. There is a small church in the city center of Moscow, St. Cosmas and Damian. Only two years ago it was still a printing shop. The people of the church are busy restoring it, as do most of the Russian Orthodox congregations. But in this church there is a special spirit. In the worship service people take their responsibilities seriously. There is no scripture reading without an explanation. The whole building is full of activities in the fields of teaching, social work, and creative arts. The core group of this church are the followers of the late Father Alexander Men. He was a Russian Orthodox priest who was assassinated four years ago. After a long time of almost total disconnection between the church and the intellectual world, he was one of the first to find the ears and the hearts of the "intelligentsia." A taxi driver in Moscow told me how Father Alexander was leading him to a vital faith in Jesus Christ. Four years ago this group opened a night university that tries to bridge the gap between Christianity and the post-Communist society. Those

stories are not yet many, but they could be told in several areas and in several denominations in Russia.

(7) *What does Methodist evangelism mean in this situation?* I sometimes surprise good Methodist people who come to Moscow to do "hands-on" mission in building The United Methodist Church in Russia when I tell them that I do not see our major evangelistic task as that of having as many United Methodist churches in Russia as possible and as soon as possible. However, to help as many persons as possible to find a vital faith in Christ, a challenge to share it, and a spiritual home—this is genuine evangelism. One of the strengths of older Methodist evangelism was to discern between the call to accept Christ and the invitation into the membership rolls of the church. Older Methodists never saw these as unrelated. They did not recruit members for a spiritualized non-institutional "church invisible," but at least in the European context, many fruits of Methodist evangelism have been harvested in other churches. In our times of a renewed denominationalism and confessionalism it would be a noble task to remind ourselves and others that evangelism is aiming higher than our institutions. Our ancestors called it the "Kingdom of God." We may talk with modesty but no less endeavor about the servant-discipleship of the servant-Lord, "that the world may believe."

CHAPTER 10

Evangelism in the Marketplace

Woodie W. White

EVANGELISM IS for me a personal witness. I cannot speak or write dispassionately about evangelism or evangelization. The center of evangelism is the telling of the story of Jesus Christ as one's own salvation story. What Christ has done, is doing, and will yet do is always the focus of our witness, while at the same time the personal faith story is the source of the motivation for that witness. A popular gospel song declares: "God is not through with me yet!" Even to those who "tell the old, old story," there are always new dimensions of how God yet surprises us. Evangelistic witness is always rooted in the story of God's grace in Jesus Christ and always points to that story. The imperative for sharing that story is in the warp and woof of our own story. The story of Jesus is good news because it is true, and this is no abstraction.

The Gospel Really Is Good News

A recent book captures the surprise of the gospel: *The Good News Is the Bad News Is Wrong*.[1] The "bad news" does not need definition. "Bad news" is experientially real for all. What, then, is the good news? The church may have made it a cliche, but for John it was fact:

> For God so loved the world that he gave his only Son, so that everyone who believes in him may not perish but may have eternal life. (John 3:16)

All else in the gospel story stands on that promise. This remains the compelling core of what Fox and Morris call "Faith-Sharing."[2] Remove this message—God's love for the world, God's gift of Jesus Christ, and God's promise—and evangelism is rendered hollow indeed. Remove this message and evangelism and what is left is strikingly similar to any organization seeking recruits. There may be many good reasons for becoming a Christian and sharing in the life and mission of the congregation, but the one unique reason is the divine indicative—"God so loved the world"—and the divine promise—"may not perish but may have eternal life."

The questions posed to a Christian missionary are also appropriately addresses to the contemporary evangelist:

> Sir, would you please tell me why these people should be Christian? Why should you tell them about your God? What right do you have to change them?[3]

And, boldly, in the face of such challenge, Matthew's Gospel presents the Great Commission:

> Go therefore and make disciples of all nations, baptizing them in the name of the Father and of the Son and of the Holy Spirit, and teaching them to obey everything that I have commanded you. And remember, I am with you always, to the end of the age. (Matt. 28:19-20)

Note the grammatical structure of the Great Commission. It is one, whole, compound sentence. The comma and the conjunction are crucial. "Making disciples" and "baptizing" are central to the evangelistic task, but equally important are "teaching" and "obeying." "Making," "baptizing," "teaching," and "obeying" are the essential functions of evangelistic witness. These injunctions of the Great Commission are what compel us to hold together evangelism and social action. In fact "evangelism and social action" are not two, but evangelism is Christian witness in word and deed. E. Stanley Jones once remarked:

> Evangelism without social action is like a soul without a body; social action without evangelism is like a body without a soul. One is a ghost and the other is a corpse. We don't want either. We must keep evangelism and social action together. Then we have a living organism.[4]

Yet, such a command, if it does not carry with it some firsthand testimony, what and how the message and Christ have impacted the bearer, will hardly be convincing. Another old gospel song sums up the matter: "I can't keep it to myself—what the Lord has done for me!" Herein is the reason why one cannot speak dispassionately about evangelism. We simply cannot keep the story to ourselves!

The North Indiana Annual Conference in its vision statement says in part that it will be a Conference with a "Passion for Jesus and a Passion for People." The scriptural admonition is pointedly correct that not only will one perish without a vision, but without a passion for that vision the vision itself will perish. Local churches and the connectional system lack not a vision (nor a plan, nor a program) but a passion. The gospel song has both the vision and the passion:

> I can't keep it to myself—
> What the Lord has done for me!
> What the Lord has done for you!
> What the Lord has done for them!
> What the Lord is doing there.
> What the Lord is doing here.
> And what the Lord is yet to do!

While the context of living faith is utterly personal, it is by no means privatistic. I am privileged to travel globally, and mass communication has enabled me to "travel" to lands where I have never physically visited. It is the local and global intersecting of my life with others—those near, those of other nations, cultures, races, and ethnic groups—that has focused my thinking, informed my world view, and gives adequate evidence of what the Lord can and is doing. "I can't keep it to myself . . . !"

The Context of Evangelism

The good news is always contextual. Its message remains the same, but the manner in which that message is shared may vary. If the good news is to be heard, understood, grasped, accepted, lived out, the bearer must have some sense of the context in which the message is shared. Three specific contexts in the sharing of the good news will be highlighted in what follows: (1) good news to the poor; (2) good news to the marginalized; and (3) good news to the prosperous.

The context of the last years of the twentieth century is aptly characterized by Charles Dickens' description of another era:

> It was the best of times, it was the worst of times, it was the age of wisdom, it was the age of foolishness, it was the epoch of belief, it was the epoch of incredulity, it was the season of Light, it was the

season of Darkness, it was the spring of hope, it was the winter of despair, we had everything before us, we had nothing before us, we were all going direct to heaven, we were all going directly the other way.[5]

The marks of the old age are still blatantly visible to us: war, famine, hate, ill will, intolerance, greed, selfishness—and sin! These paradoxical times are the context of our evangelism—our faith sharing. In such paradoxical times the late preacher and social reformer, George MacLeod of Glasgow and Iona, observed thirty years ago:

> I simply argue that the Cross be raised again at the center of the marketplace, as well as on the steeple of the church. I am recovering the claim that Jesus was not crucified in a Cathedral between two candles, but on a Cross between two thieves; on a town garbage heap; on a crossroads so cosmopolitan that they had to write his title in Hebrew and Latin and in Greek; at the kind of place where cynics talk smut, and thieves curse, and soldiers gamble. Because that is where He died and this is what He died about. And that is where churchmen should be and what churchmen should be about.[6]

Noninclusive language aside, this was and is the context of evangelism—the open marketplace, not the secure church! Yet it is here that we increasingly are the most uncomfortable.

Our reluctance to enter the marketplace is countered with John Wesley's own words and ministry. In our time the marketplace is what the open fields were in Wesley's time. Initially, Wesley also was reluctant. On April 1, 1739, he heard George Whitefield preach in the open air. Whitefield was urging the same practice with Wesley. Wesley wrote in his *Journal*:

> I could scarce reconcile myself at first to this *strange way* of preaching in the fields . . . having been all my life (till very lately) so tenacious of every point relating to decency and order, that I should have thought the saving of souls *almost a sin* if it had not been done *in a church.*[7]

That following day Wesley began his evangelistic venture of preaching in the fields appropriately taking his text from the Sermon on the Mount, entering in his *Journal* this description: "I begun expounding our Lord's Sermon on the Mount (one pretty remarkable precedent of *field preaching*, though I suppose *there were churches* at that time also) to a little society which was accustomed to meet once or twice a week in Nicholas Street."[8] The contemporary church may seek the comfort of seclusion, but, pray God, we will be haunted by the vision of Jesus on the mount and Wesley on the plain. In the contemporary marketplace people are caught in the self-compulsive logic of getting ahead while keeping others back. People are victimized by poverty while others savor their possessions. Paradoxically, compulsive hedonism and compulsive despair are equally present in the marketplace. The logic of the gospel is a different logic, and millions of people will hear it only in the marketplace.

Good News to the Poor

Methodism began as an evangelistic movement among the poor. Wesley appraised his movement with these words:

> And surely never in any age or nation, since the Apostles have those words been so eminently fulfilled, "the poor have the gospel preached unto them," as it is at this day.[9]

In the West the people called Methodists have gradually become negligent in following Wesley's example. If there is any segment in our society where as a denomination we have been wanting in our evangelistic task, it is with the poor. In other parts of the world the picture is different. Yet in this country the poor are hardly present among us. If the poor are not within the church, unmistakably their presence pervades the marketplace. What is indisputable is the fact that we have failed in our evangelistic task with the poor. For we either run from the poor, hide from them, or ignore them! As the major metropolitan and rural areas become economically more desperate, strangely United Methodism's presence begins to disappear from these same marketplaces of desperation. We cannot evangelize where we are not!

Increasingly we are not found where the poor are. We sell our churches or give them away, move to different territory, and thereby continue to place a distance between "them" and "us." It is not at all uncommon for a United Methodist congregation to sit in the middle of a community of poverty and be surrounded by empty pews. Then upon fleeing the community, the same building and the same pews are filled with people who are converts of others' evangelistic efforts. The homogeneous principle of church growth has convinced us, or so it seems, that we can only be faith bearers among the prosperous, the "up and coming" or only those like ourselves. Yet Methodism was most fruitful in its evangelistic efforts when those with a missionary spirit were willing to share the good news in settings alien, new, and different.

If we are to evangelize among the poor, to share the good news, we must be willing to listen to the poor, learn from the poor, live with the poor, and stand with the poor. It is the poor who can demonstrate to us how to make the good news message hearable and believable in their context. Understandably we "do church" and evangelism the way we know best, rather than learn from the poor how evangelistic witness is done in that particular context.

The church itself may experience a revival when it joins with the poor. Bishop Kenneth Carder's judgment is both Wesleyan and contemporary when he observes:

> Recovery of an ongoing, personal relationship with the poor may be the best means of proclaiming the gospel of grace in this age. Wesley believed the biblical theme that God is among the poor. It is the poor who strip us of our idols of self-sufficiency, achievement, and success and put us in touch with grace.[10]

Good News to the Marginalized

There are many "politically correct" definitions of the marginalized. Such a definition is not offered here. Rather, simply stated, the marginalized are those who are ignored, rejected, stereotyped, pushed into an amorphous crowd, consigned to the sidelines while the big game goes on. These are commonly called the marginalized. Marginalization is a process which goes on in and beyond the categories of class, race, gender, and age.

Here I am concerned primarily with the church as a *marginalizer*. The marginalized are all those who are intentionally or unintentionally kept out of our circle of faith and fellowship. They are the ones who feel unwelcome, unloved, unwanted, and unappreciated. Increasingly they are those who hold different political or even theological opinions whether conservative, liberal, evangelical, or social activist.

The marginalized are "strangers in the kingdom." The plot of an intriguing novel is set in beautiful Vermont. The story unfolds as the village church calls a new minister from Canada to be its pastor. After a long period without a pastor, the congregation is eager to have at long last a spiritual leader again. So impressed are they with one candidate's impeccable credentials, excellent recommendations, and exciting telephone interview that they decide to call him without the normal meeting with the search committee. Only after the new pastor arrives do the townspeople and congregation learn that their new pastor is Black. The name of the town is Kingdom. The title of the book is *A Stranger in the Kingdom*.[11]

There are many strangers in the "Kingdom." For a host of reasons the "faithful" do not share the good news with them. One embarrassingly fundamental reason is that the "faithful" have themselves made others "strangers" or marginalized ones. The logic of universal grace, the message that Christ died for all, is irrefutable. We cannot refuse to share. When we do refuse, we marginalize others and contradict the gospel.

In every community there are the marginalized waiting to hear the liberating word of the gospel. So much of our evangelistic schemes and outreach seem to be socially grounded rather than theologically grounded. What seems more important is the sociological identity and not the theological identity—a person in need of God's grace and salvation in Jesus Christ. In today's climate where "labels" are becoming more important than persons, the church is "marginalizing" itself out of significant evangelistic opportunities. Every congregation in every community should examine itself to determine whom it has marginalized. The United Methodist Church as a connectional system must ask: Whom we have marginalized? The gospel must be for everyone or it is for no one! For whom did Christ not die?

Good News to the Prosperous

As conventionally interpreted, the words of Jesus seem to convey only faint hope for the prosperous: "Truly I tell you, it will be hard for a rich person to enter the kingdom of heaven" (Matt. 19:23). Perhaps Jesus understood the false sense of security that possessions often create. Certainly Jesus understood the attracting power of material goods. Note carefully, however, Jesus does not marginalize or exclude the prosperous. On one occasion he looked lovingly upon a "rich young man." He did not decline or run away from the invitation to hospitality in Zacchaeus' house.

Sometimes the church falsely perceives that the rich and prosperous are complete, totally satisfied, needing neither God nor others.

Sometimes the non-rich can idolize acquisition and wealth as much as the prosperous. Certainly with good Jewish background, Jesus never proposed that somehow the material world should be equated with evil or that evil was inherent within the material. No one who takes seriously the Judeo-Christian understanding of creation can forget the fundamental conviction of the goodness of creation including all that is earthy and material. The locus of evil is not in matter but in the mind or heart of the morally accountable human agent.

Likewise, Christians cannot ignore the universal inclusivity of the gospel. The grace of God is abundantly available to rich and poor alike. The efficacious work of grace is always versatile, differing according to the conditions of every human situation. God's grace works differently among the poor and the prosperous, always to the end that all may know the abundant life, the new creation in Christ. Both the prosperous and the impoverished need the good news, maybe for varying penultimate reasons, but both alike for the ultimate reason that Jesus Christ is "the way, the truth, and the life."

The plain truth is that many economically secure people experience constantly the opposite of security. Speaking for many modern men and women, a social commentator of Christian sensitivity has recently observed:

> Work and money are too central to our lives to be divorced from the values and assumptions of our faith. We need the guidance and the moral strength to make hard decisions—about cutting back when we find our work stealing too much of our energy, about difficult ethical questions at work, about our consumer spending, and about ways to be of service to others. We also need guidance and moral strength in thinking about the pervasive materialism of our society, the huge disparities between rich and poor; and the ministries of our churches and charitable organizations.[12]

Modern women and men do not need to be made to feel guilty about their possessions in order to be "won" to Christ. They already sense a gnawing ethical dilemma. Many times they experience this dilemma as being caught in a consumerist system of which they seemingly have little power to correct. The evangelical invitation is not prefaced by a series of laws or maxims calculated to freeze the prosperous in a state of helpless passivity. The evangelical invitation is to "come, see a man" who offers a new world of reality which is the kingdom of God. The evangelical invitation is to a community of moral discourse (the church) composed of persons who in faith endeavor to be on the discipleship way to the Kingdom.

To be honest, in some ways United Methodists actually have proven to be successful in reaching the prosperous. Our churches are largely middle and upper-middle class, especially in the United States. Many times we have offered them nothing more than trinkets. The array of programming offered in many churches looks more like a social services market. Many so-called secular people may respond to our ecclesiastical commodities, when really there are profoundly deeper needs within and around them. Some may not know it for they may well believe their own "press clippings" about themselves. Yet, when the clamor subsides, they experience the same sense of futility and emptiness which others who are less economically fortunate face. Indeed the prosperous may be the more confused because it is assumed that riches bring wholeness, meaning and happiness. The irony is that many are rich but feel poor!

Conclusion

Christian witness in the marketplace is the responsibility of the whole church. We dare not leave this awesome responsibility in the hands of a few specialists, clergy, or board of directors. If the good news is to be shared in the marketplace with the poor, the marginalized, and the prosperous, it will be the responsibility of the whole church.

L. Harold DeWolf, one of the leading theologians of our church in recent years, once wrote:

> In the church today, we often wonder how we can get priests and ministers into factory, office, home, legislative committee, and council of state to speak the reconciling word of God. Yet all the while we have priests and ministers in all those places! For every man or woman who has been reconciled to God through Christ has been called of God to be a minister of this reconciling word wherever he lives and works.[13]

A major responsibility of the church is to provide the opportunity for persons to be molded and shaped by the gospel so that they are equipped to render this diaconal ministry in the world.

Presently many of our churches manifest a passive attitude about the marketplace and content themselves with a ministry of institutional maintenance. At the same time, the marketplace presents itself as the mission field of the church. The church needs to move from a "reverse gear" mentality to an active "forward gear" engagement. Leonard Sweet graphically illustrates the contrast and challenge:

> Frogs sit and wait until their food walks, flies, or swims past. Then they pounce. Lizards go out in search of food. In the frog world, everything comes to those who wait. In the lizard world, everyone would die if they sat and waited. The postmodern climate is not conducive to frog ministries. "Come-to" strategies no longer work. It's a "go-to" world.[14]

It has never been otherwise for people genuinely empowered by the gospel of grace.

CHAPTER 11

Intellectual Challenges to the Gospel

Kenneth L. Carder

BELIEF IN AND COMMITMENT TO a transcendent other who is graciously present and active in the world has always confronted intellectual challenges. From the bewildered Moses standing beside a mysterious talking, burning bush asking for God's name, to the prophets trying to make sense of the two seemingly contradictory poles of divine chosenness and national collapse, to the pious Job struggling to trust in a good and loving God while enduring unfair sufferings, people of faith have had to face formidable intellectual challenges.

The church's evangelistic mandate inevitably includes apologetics. Jesus' proclamation of the dawning of a new world immediately conflicted with the mindset of an old world. The early church met the challenge of interpreting the nature and work of Jesus Christ in the context of long held and variant Jewish traditions as well as Hellenistic culture, whose heroes were mythological figures and Greek philosophers, not suffering servants or Hebrew prophets.

Throughout history the great spiritual revivals and periods of institutional reform and renewal have come as the church confronted or was confronted with significant questioning of conventional wisdom and popular practice. Martin Luther launched a religious revolution by nailing ninety-five theological theses to the door at Wittenberg. The Reformation emerged from the vigorous theological probing and proclamation by such towering intellectuals as Luther, Calvin, and Zwingli.

John Wesley and the eighteenth century Methodists were England's most effective Christian apologists and evangelists for the gospel. It was an era of growing rationalism, runaway hedonism, and creeping adventurous individualism. Paradigms were shifting as the

Enlightenment expanded the role and place of reason, science, industrialization, and urbanization. The Wesleyan wedding of knowledge and piety, reason and emotion, intellectual vigor and evangelical zeal represented an alternative to arid rationalism and undisciplined or unreasoned emotionalism.

The heirs of Wesley in the late years of the twentieth century confront an era of waning rationalism, bankrupt hedonism, and individualism turned into madness and meanness. The church now faces the demise of the Enlightenment's influence.[1] Paradigms produced by the age of reason are crumbling, and the church today must proclaim the gospel in a "between-time era." It may, however, be a *kairos* moment, since the gospel itself is the best hope for the shaping of a new paradigm.

Obstacles to Confronting Intellectual Challenges

Intellectual challenges to the gospel have been met with varied responses by the church. Violent resistance and ecclesiastical defensiveness have been prevalent means of silencing inquisitive and dissenting voices. Coercion always seems to be a more readily available weapon against heresy than persuasion. Withdrawal into intellectually homogeneous enclaves of doctrinal purity is always a temptation of the intellectually challenged. Carefully crafted, unambiguous creedal statements fashioned into legislative mandates and used as weapons to be hurled at inquisitors continues as a popular, abortive attempt to meet contemporary intellectual challenges.

Acquiescence and uncritical capitulation are popular means of avoiding the apologetic and evangelistic mandates of the gospel. Rather than critiquing popular cultural paradigms in the light of the gospel, the gospel is made compatible with the culture. The unexamined values of the prevailing culture replace the reality, nature, presence, and action of God as the foundation of the church's existence. The community entrusted with the gospel loses any significant historical presence by blurring the radical distinctiveness between the reign of God and the world as it is. Such a church equates evangelism with membership growth, discipleship with institutional maintenance, and mission with programmatic options.

American Methodists have a long history of avoiding challenges to the gospel by adopting a stubborn anti-intellectualism. John Wesley, who squarely and intentionally took on the challenges to the gospel by his Enlightenment contemporaries, exhibited an intellectual rigorousness and theological intensity lacking on the American frontier. There an anti-intellectualism took root, and the marriage between knowledge and piety has always been strained. Peter Cartwright in the nineteenth century countered the intellectuals with fervor and humor. When he was taunted by a seminary graduate who wanted to know why the Methodists didn't have any Doctors of Divinity among them, Cartwright retorted, "Humph, our divinity ain't sick, don't need no doctrin'."[2] My own grandmother, who taught in a Methodist Sunday school, advised when she learned that I was going to seminary, "Don't let those professors take away your faith."

Anti-intellectualism, acquiescence and capitulation, and violent resistance and ecclesiastical defensiveness have severely crippled the church's witness in this in-between-time era. The gospel has been trivialized and marginalized by the society and the church. Theology rarely appears in the public discussion of societal issues. God has become an unnecessary option, even in the church which relies more on the programmatic strategies than the power of the gospel. Theology, once the queen of the sciences, is no longer seen as a science; and it exists behind the walls of academia where it is ignored or even scorned by the church, which considers theology as less foundational than sociology, psychology, and marketing. Clergy, therefore, are more concerned about how to run a church than how to know and serve God. The tough questions raised by a world dominated by science, technology, and economics go unaddressed. Religious faith becomes privatized, compartmentalized, relativized, and trivialized. The challenges confronting the world as a result of the waning influence of the Enlightenment paradigms go unanswered by the community of Christ, which always lives in-between-times.

The time, however, is right for The United Methodist Church to confront the challenge. Having deep roots in the Enlightenment and the evangelical revival, we have a tradition and ethos which God can use again to reform the continents and spread scriptural holiness throughout the lands.

Meeting the Intellectual Challenges of the Enlightenment

A world that looks to science, technology, economics, and politics for salvation represents a formidable challenge to the proclamation of salvation as a gift from a gracious, loving God. Recovery of the nature and power of the gospel by a church which has been shaped by the paradigms of the Enlightenment begins with honest repentance of idolatry. Having pursued the gods of cause-and-effect rationalism, quantifiable empiricism, and expansionist consumerism, the church now suffers from theological amnesia and missional anemia. The church has been stripped of the very resource necessary for confronting the challenges of a postmodern world—the gospel, the good news of God's decisive victory in Jesus Christ over the powers of sin and death.

The demise of the Enlightenments paradigms of cause-and-effect science, inevitable progress through knowledge, truth as verifiable facts, power as created energy, the superiority of the human species, history as accumulated human experiences, and mystery as merely a gap in knowledge provides a fertile context for rigorous theological reflection and accountable evangelical zeal.

The challenges are real and they demand the best thinking possible by all segments of the contemporary church. Confronting the challenges requires that we put aside our political agendas, our ecclesiastical defensiveness, and our institutional protectionism and grapple with essential components of the gospel in the context of this post-Enlightenment era.

The Finality of Jesus Christ

Central to the gospel is the affirmation that Jesus Christ is the supreme incarnate manifestation of God's nature, purpose, and presence. The Enlightenment paradigm resists such a central affirmation of the finality of Christ. A church shaped by the Enlightenment paradigm has been hesitant to proclaim the supremacy of Jesus Christ in a pluralistic world of variant religious traditions. The democratization of Christianity reduces Jesus Christ from Sovereign and Lord to another option among the multitude of culturally determined religious expressions. D. T. Niles put it succinctly:

> The crux of the finality issue is whether or not in Jesus Christ [people] confront and are confronted by the transcendent God whose will they cannot manipulate, by whose judgment they are bound, and with whose intractable presence in their midst they must inevitably reckon.[3]

Is Jesus Christ the supreme incarnate revelation of God or isn't he?

If he is, then we must listen to him, understand him, follow him, and be the means by which the world is transformed by him.

The Enlightenment exposed the fallacy of proclaiming the finality of Christ by a coercive religious imperialism under the guise of evangelism and missionary zeal. The finality of Jesus Christ is no justification for cultural genocide or a religious form of colonialism. Christological rhetoric and creedal formulations cannot be substituted for the reality which took on flesh in Jesus of Nazareth. Salvation in and through Jesus Christ means far more than mental and verbal assent to Christological affirmations. The missionary and evangelistic enterprises are replete with denials of the reality of Jesus Christ in the name of loyalty to Jesus Christ.

What does it mean to affirm the sovereignty of Christ in a world in which less than 25 percent of the people consider themselves to be Christian? How can salvation through Jesus Christ alone be preached with integrity when the majority of the world's people accept no such claim and live wholesome, full lives apart from any explicit reference to Jesus Christ?

Further, what does the sovereignty of Christ mean in the context of a scientific world view which assumes the supremacy of natural law and ecological systems? Is Christ sovereign over creation as Paul's Letter to the Colossians claims (1:15-20), or is Christ relegated to the narrow compartment of religion where sovereignty is limited to interior pious feelings or private morality? What are the implications of the finality of Jesus Christ in a society of moral and ethical relativism?

Any bold proclamation of the gospel will require facing squarely and honestly the meaning and implication of the finality of Jesus Christ. Otherwise the gospel becomes but another option available in the market place of religious ideas, the validity of which is determined by the sincerity of the believer. Such a relativized gospel has no compelling power to shape a new paradigm. It is but the vestiges of a waning rationalism.[4]

God's Reign Over Creation

At the heart of the Christian gospel is this message: "Jesus came to Galilee, proclaiming the good news of God, and saying, 'The time is fulfilled, and the kingdom of God has come near; repent, and believe the good news" (Mark 1:14-15). In Jesus Christ God brought near a new world. God's power, God's presence, God's purposes invaded the world and triumphed over the powers of sin and death. The kingdom of God represents a shift in paradigm from an old world dominated by sin and death to a new world dominated by grace and resurrection. In the life, teaching, death, resurrection and ascension of Jesus Christ a new creation came into being. A new world dawned and the Christ event represents a sign and foretaste of the future God intends to bring. The Kingdom has come but it is still to come. The gospel keeps alive both the memory of God's mighty acts in Jesus Christ and the expectation of the consummation of God's reign over creation.

Absent from the gospel as preached in United Methodist churches in the modern world are eschatology and teleology. The Enlightenment replaced providence with history and divine expectancy with scientific extrapolation. Eschatology was left to the apocalyptic fringes, otherworldly speculation, and pious escapism from the real world. Hope hinged on scientific, technological, economic, and political triumphalism. Even the kingdom of God became something humans could build, manage, and institutionalize. Visions of the future are shaped more by the politics of self-interest and economics than by the good news of a new heaven and a new earth. Talk of vision in the contemporary United Methodist Church sounds more like a cheer designed to rally a dying institution than a clarion announcement of God's victory over sin and death. The church conforms more to the values of a success oriented culture than it conforms to the image of God's vision for creation.

The world is shaped by expectation and vision as well as by memory. A vision of what ought to be shapes science, technology, economics, and politics. Eschatology and teleology, therefore, are as determinative as sociology and biology. Our vision of the meaning and end toward which creation moves is as determinative as our memory of what has been. The omission of eschatology and teleology from the story reduces the gospel to a satisfying solution to personal problems and a means to selfish ends. Happiness, peace of mind, and success become the signs of divine favor. Salvation requires nothing more than self-acceptance and a support group.

The postmodern world suffers from lack of vision. In the absence of a comprehensive vision a narrow politically motivated agenda is emerging. It is dominated by fear, special interest ideologies, and the economic security of the privileged. God's vision of a healed creation and a reconciled humanity has been obliterated from the public agenda. Efforts to fashion a world of justice, compassion, and righteousness seem naive, even irrelevant, to a people focused on personal security, happiness, and peace of mind.

Globalization, then, represents a formidable challenge to and opportunity for the affirmation of God's reign over creation. The gospel, with its paradigm of a new heaven and a new earth transformed by the lordship of Jesus Christ, represents a vision capable of shaping a postmodern world. Meeting the challenge requires that eschatology and teleology return to the church's life and message.

Community and Ecclesiology

The postmodern era is experiencing the consequences of an idolatrous individualism. The collapse of community may represent the last gasp of an individualism spawned by the Enlightenment's paradigms of individual freedom and human potential. The elevation of personal, individual rights above the health and wholeness of community results in isolation, loneliness, violence, and exploitation. Coupled with the market logic of exchange, individualism reduces everything and everyone to a commodity to be used for the self-defined ends of the powerful. Political and economic power is concentrated in the hands of the few; and the Biblical notion of justice as the incorporation of the poor, the strangers and sojourners, into community is dismissed.

The gospel is personal and social, individual and communal. From the calling of Abraham and Sarah to the gift of the Holy Spirit at Pentecost, God has been about the business of bringing into being a community shaped and empowered by God's presence. In Jesus Christ God reconciled the world unto Godself and called a community to be the agent of reconciliation (2 Cor. 5:16–21).

The church exists to be a sign, forestaste, and instrument of God's new community. As a Christ-shaped community, the church resists homogeneity and practices hospitality, especially to the strangers. It seeks to live now in the light of God's final victory over sin and death; and in so doing the church is a contra-cultural movement. Although a part of the culture, the church keeps alive the vision of another world, an alternative community in which acceptance and worth are based on God's gift of grace, not on the market logic of exchange.

A major intellectual challenge to the gospel is the meaning of community amid racial, cultural, religious, and socioeconomic diversity. How is the church to be both a compassionate community and community's conscience? What does it mean to hold people accountable and hold them in love? What new forms of congregational life are needed in order to practice hospitality in the midst of racial and socioeconomic alienation? How can the American church receive the gifts of the poor and marginalized?

Ecclesiology, then, represents a major challenge to the contemporary church. The United Methodist Church in America suffers from an ecclesiology shaped more by secular sociology and corporate bureaucracy than by Christian theology and missional commitment. The result is what one church historian has called "ecclesiocracy without ecclesiology."[5] High on the agenda of the church's challenge is an ecclesiology rooted in the gospel and lived in the context of a global community.

Recovering the Centrality of Theology

If The United Methodist Church is to meet the intellectual challenge of the gospel in an in-between-time, theology must be central to the church's life, structure, and mission. The critical questions confronting the world are theological: Who is God? What is God doing? and What is the world's response to the nature and action of God?

Rigorous theological discipline and exploration have been marginalized, even by the church. As an academic discipline, theology has become more a consideration of what others *think about* God than a means of *knowing* God and thinking theologically. Theologians find their identity and accountability in professional guilds more than in faith communities; and few of their works are read outside academia. The institutional church's agencies, bureaucracies, leaders, and pastors rely on sociology and psychology, rather than on theology; and it is now possible to build a large, prosperous religious institution without belief in God.

Meeting the intellectual challenge to the gospel in a post-Enlightenment era requires that every Christian take up the theological task. Bishops and district superintendents must give priority to the teaching office of the episcopacy. The building of bridges between the institutional church and the seminaries is a needed first step. The presence of theologians from the seminaries at meetings of the

Council of Bishops is as necessary as the presence of agency staff and lawyers. Ongoing theological studies and reflection by bishops and cabinets, using the best scholarship available, must inform and critique all administrative and programmatic activity. The language and grammar of the gospel must dominate our institutional life, not the language and grammar of a world shaped by the paradigms of pragmatic secularism.

If the church is to rise to the intellectual challenge of a postmodern age, pastors will need to see themselves as theologians. Helping people know God is more important than learning how to run a successful church. Preaching, teaching, pastoral care, and ordering of church life must be rooted in God's vision for the world as revealed in Jesus Christ. The pastor's tasks are the proclamation of an alternative way of viewing the world and the nurturing of communities which reflect God's reign over creation. The tasks are theological; they center in who God is, what God is doing, and the appropriate response to God's being and doing.

Theology in the postmodern world involves dialogue—with the tradition, the culture, and the emerging paradigms. Crucial to the dialogue is the awareness that the world no longer thinks in theological categories. As Leander Keck has reminded us in *The Church Confident*, the challenge is no longer faith in search of understanding; it is understanding in search of faith.[6] Nevertheless, the deep longings to which the gospel speaks are real. Identifying the non-theological categories in which the need for the gospel is expressed represents one of the intellectual challenges awaiting the contemporary evangelist. Shifting from paradigms dominated by the Enlightenment's rationalism, empiricism, and individualism to paradigms shaped by the finality of Jesus Christ, the reign of God over creation, and community formed by God's vision for humanity requires rigorous theological discipline by all Christians.

Conclusion

United Methodists stand in a tradition which includes balance between knowledge and piety, personal assurance and social witness, holiness of heart and corporate righteousness, evangelical zeal and missional commitment. John Wesley diligently defended and courageously proclaimed the gospel during an age of shifting world views. His theological apologetics and evangelical proclamation contributed to the forming of new paradigms. For him, defense of the gospel was a serious matter. He persistently critiqued the emerging scientific world view in the light of the historic doctrines of the church and he was well versed in the literature, philosophy, and problems of eighteenth-century English culture. He held before the masses, especially the poor and marginalized, a vision of life as prevenient, justifying, and sanctifying grace.

The waning years of the twentieth century present to the heirs of Wesley formidable intellectual challenges. The post-Enlightenment world awaits the formation of new paradigms, a new perception of reality. The gospel meets the challenge of a new world. The gospel is about a new world God has revealed in Jesus Christ. It is a new heaven and a new earth forged by redeeming and reconciling grace. Since God has already won the final victory, we can live now in terms of the finality of Jesus Christ, God's reign over creation, and a new community in which the risen Christ lives and serves.

CHAPTER 12

The Global Gospel

Alfred L. Norris

CHRISTIANITY IS a missionary religion. It had its beginnings as a movement composed of impassioned, zealous converts who wanted to share their new life in Christ with others. Their desire to make Christ known was further mandated by his (Christ's) commission, commonly called the "Great Commission."[1] Arias and Johnson suggest that it might be called the "Final Commission," the "Last Mandate," the "Mission Charge," or the "Last Commission," instead of the "Great Commission."[2]

Early Christian missionaries were hard working, self-sacrificing, and humble, willing to decrease so that Christ would be increased, to be abased in order for Christ to be exalted. The gospel they proclaimed was a salvific one and the encouragement they offered was well received. Our beloved United Methodism, through its predecessor denominations, took seriously the missionary impetus and began to do Christian evangelism outside the United States in the mid-nineteenth century. Its primary emphasis was, initially, on personal conversion.

With the passage of time a different method and style were employed as Eurocentrism, arrogance, and paternalism came to be seen as characterizing the evangelistic endeavors of American Christians. There was seemingly little or no concern or respect for the social, cultural, or economic conditions of the peoples whom they were interested in disciplining. The Eurocentrism is understandable; the arrogance and paternalism less so. All of us are products of our own cultures, lifestyles, language, environment, and history. But to assume that differences denote superiority or inferiority is, at best, laden with deception.

In this essay I propose to explore three factors that affect the globalization of the Christian gospel, namely, cross-cultural communication, contextualization, and inculturation. This triad presents challenges which began to surface over the last two decades and are mounting in intensity with each passing day. To ignore or minimize any or all of them is to risk endangering the effectiveness of the evangelistic enterprise in terms of its global appeal. Indeed, these concerns have contributed to a change in the *modus operandi* of Christian evangelism.

Cross-Cultural Communication

One of the lessons of life, painfully learned, is that communication is a two-way street. One must talk, but also listen; teach, but also learn. This cannot be accomplished unless there is openness and mutual respect.

The Western world, because of its technological advances and modernization, historically found it difficult to refrain from a posture of superiority and almost total disregard for the opinions of developing nations, for example. That picture is changing as nations and peoples begin to assert themselves by demanding and gaining their independence. Much of this is due to trade, travel, and satellite communications. It is normally less difficult for two or more free persons or nations to communicate with each other than is the case when one is free and the other is servant. To some extent the economic and political realities of our time are bold testimonies of a new day in international communication and cooperation.

In the sphere of religion it has long been the belief and practice of Christianity that salvation is not possible except through Jesus Christ. How that is communicated to and with cultures, and whether they accept or dispute it, forms the basis for cross-cultural religious understanding.

Religion, in some form or expression, has been a part of the human experience from the beginning. Even those who denounce the Christian's God believe in and proclaim, what is for them, a suitable substitute. This fact alone should give us hope rather than drive us to the brink of despair. We can begin to design and fashion dialogical models of cross-cultural possibilities based on the premise that every culture, domestic or foreign, is a basically religious one. To write off large percentages of the human family as "heathen" because they have not accepted Jesus Christ as Savior and Lord is to exemplify one's own disloyalty to him. The zenith of anti-Christian behavior is reached when the Christian fears or refuses dialogue with persons of differing religious persuasions.

It is not inconceivable that some religions are Christ-influenced if not Christ-centered. Christ is not the dominant, all-consuming force, but many of the precepts of Christ are honored in their religious quest. This was brought sharply into focus when the Parliament of the World's Religions gathered in Chicago August 18–September 5, 1993. Some six thousand religious leaders and faithful, representing one hundred twenty-five faiths from around the world, caused some to describe the event as "the greatest gathering of religious and spiritual leaders in history." The participants came together

> . . . to celebrate a common longing and to recommit the world's religions to work together to solve the planet's many problems including seemingly pandemic violence, population growth, AIDS and spreading ecological ruin. Many expressed the view that it was none too soon for the world's religious leaders to rededicate themselves to common effort.[3]

Whenever religious people, of whatever culture, give attention to concerns that are common and affect all humankind, cross-cultural communication is not only possible but desirable. Experiences can either unite or divide. When these experiences are shared they induce a unanimity of interest and a concerted effort to improve conditions.

We do well to remind ourselves that the creation story in the book of Genesis is highly descriptive of God's plan for unity within diversity. Correspondingly, when we acknowledge diversity and honor it, in some small way we honor and acknowledge God, who is the author of diversity. God called every creative act "good," so we are challenged to see goodness in diverse traditions and in peoples different from ourselves.[4]

One of the many fringe benefits of cross-cultural communication is that in learning more about diverse cultures and peoples, we inevitably deepen our appreciation of our own culture, its strengths, and places where improvements are needed. Wisdom forbids us to yield to the temptation of assuming that everything about our culture is right, whereas different mores and practices in other cultures are primitive, backward, and uncivil.

There is widespread belief that United Methodism and other mainline denominations have retreated from their traditional interest in evangelizing persons from non-Christian groups. This is no longer a priority with them. If this is true some would postulate that United Methodism has abdicated its responsibility and its missionary-evangelistic zeal. On the other hand it may signal a healthier respect and appreciation by our church for other religious expressions. Could it be that more congenial dialogue is being undertaken in an atmosphere of mutual trust and understanding? This is somewhat analogous to the denominationalism within Christendom. Few denominations place a priority on proselytizing; instead they focus their time and energies on offering Christ to the unchurched, sinners in need of salvation.

There is some validity to the notion that because of who Christ is, he is indeed the object of every religious search, even if his name is not called by those involved or included in the search. It is a contradiction in terms to say that God is love, and that God is most fully revealed in Jesus Christ, but then deny that Christ loves all people, Christian and Jew, Hindu and Buddhist, Confucianist and Muslim. If he loves them, God makes it possible for them to love him, though sometimes via a different cultural expression. This view allows us to conclude that whenever, however, or wherever people worship, Christ is present.

Nearly forty years ago a leading authority on the world's religions captured the essence of the omnipresence of Christ when he penned these thoughts:

> Because he loves all [people], he stands beside the Hindu chanting mantras and bowing his head at his shrine. He lingers beside the Jew reading the Torah . . . he pauses beside the Parsi bowing to the sacred fire in his secret temple. He watches the follower of Confucius who reverently beholds the tablets of the temple, the Taoist burning incense in his golden altars, the Buddhist spinning the prayer wheels, and the Shintoist making his pilgrimages to the holy shrine. He keeps his vigil over the Muslim kneeling on his prayer rug in the mosque, and he hears the echo of the imam as he calls, "There is no God but Allah." He is interested in all sincere seekers after truth, even though they have not yet arrived at a full understanding of God.[5]

Engaging the mind, tongue and spirit of peoples of other cultures in creative dialogue is not evangelical retrenchment. It is actually a giant first step in establishing a "level playing field" that can only yield a more receptive attitude and openness to the gospel message. When one has faith in the proclaimer, one is more likely to develop faith in who is being proclaimed.

Contextualization

An incident occurred in my home state during the late 1950s or early 1960s which I remember to this day. A Caucasian clergyperson visited an African American worship service one Sunday morning. He was on vacation and decided to do something different for his spiritual enrichment. The church he visited was served by a seminary-educated pastor who was highly respected in the African American community. The African American pastor's sermon was disturbing and tremendously disappointing to the Caucasian preacher. He remarked to someone that it was disgraceful and theologically bankrupt.

A similar incident occurred during my senior year in seminary. I was enrolled in a course in contemporary theology. One day a pastor, an alumnus of the institution, paid a visit to that class. The professor welcomed him and issued him an invitation to address the class, but the pastor declined. The professor insisted, so the pastor said something like this:

> What you are studying here is far removed from the concerns of the people whom I serve. What they want to know is how they are going to pay the rent, feed their families, and educate their children. They want to hear a word from God that speaks hope to their condition.

I know both of these pastors and their churches personally. I was convinced then, and am now, that they were faithful and effective ministers of Jesus Christ who were doing ministry in the context of their history and circumstances. They were preaching and providing pastoral services to oppressed and economically and culturally challenged people.

One of the most liberating concepts that has been advanced over the years is that the Bible is always contemporary. Every message, every person, included in its pages is afforded a position of relevance in addressing some issue or culture in our contemporary world. The conviction of the relevance of the biblical message gives rise to the acceptance, even expectation, of differing interpretations of Scripture. It has always been true that what one sees, at least initially, is conditioned by one's existential perspective. Our interpretation of Scripture, and its resulting application to life situations, is influenced by the culture within which we live and move and have our being.

Contextualizing the gospel is especially challenging and extremely complex when an international culture is involved. This reality does not exempt us from the glorious opportunity and privilege of discovering creative and exciting ways of making Christ known. Leaving our cultural neighborhoods in order to help others find a transforming relationship with the Savior can be an adventure which knows no parallel.

So much is lost, and many opportunities squandered, when arguments arise between proponents of varying theological perspectives. Relegating the claims and promises of the gospel to a secondary position, while giving more prominence to theological correctness than is merited, has presented a confused and distorted appeal to men and women who are hungry for the living bread. It must be remembered that John Wesley was concerned about both personal salvation and social transformation. The poor and the outcast were beneficiaries of his theological construction and understanding. Our neat, well-appointed, and expensive theological furniture is of little import if it cannot adequately equip the evangelical condominium to house "the wretched of the earth" as well as the privileged and powerful. It is not likely that all Christians will ever embrace *one* theological posture, and that is probably a blessing. The larger question is whether one's theology helps or hinders in the proclamation of the gospel and ushering in the kingdom of God.

Great care should be exercised in overcoming the tendency to subordinate the claims of the gospel to the vagaries of culture. The Christian faith is presented and lived within the culture of its adherents, but it does not depend on the culture for its validity or authenticity. The gospel promises "abundant life." I submit that such a quality of life is transformational, and transformed lives have the power to transform society or culture. The kingdom of God is not subservient to anyone or anything. The kingdom of God is the end of all our striving—to bring the world and all its peoples and places under the rule, reign, and dominion of God. The gospel, then, transcends culture.

Eagerness to win someone over can eventuate in the use of

tactics, language, or other offensive methods which drive them away instead. If the presenter is convinced that his/her method is consistent with the urgency of the gospel, there is little chance that any alteration in the approach will be forthcoming.

It would be a mistake of the highest order to assume that all, or even most, contextual concerns are the purview of American Christians who are seeking to spread the gospel to persons in other countries exclusively. The more conservative Christian bodies deal with contextualization issues on a continuing basis because many of their converts combine a profound interest in cross-cultural questions with a deep commitment to theological orthodoxy. And this is more than a "foreign mission" question, since many "new immigrant groups have begun to bring issues of interreligious dialogue to our own doorsteps."[6]

Within every racial, ethnic, or cultural group there are differences related to age, education, and gender, to name a few. Stereotypical assignments, therefore, should be avoided at all costs. Some dynamics of a group's history, however, should not be sacrificed. This writer has agonizing memories of a time when the "Negro Spiritual" was deemphasized as an authentic religious expression and art form. Many educated and upwardly mobile Blacks were ashamed to sing their own songs because they allowed other groups to mold their psyches into a state of denial and inferiority. The task of the Christian missionary/evangelist is to translate the biblical message, the gospel, into the cultural context of the lost without compromising the truth of Scripture.

Paul G. Heibert suggests four checks against overcontextualizing the gospel. These, he contends, will help us guard against a relativism engendered by theological pluralism, or the syncretism that results from the gospel becoming captive to our cultures.[7] He lists the checkpoints as follows:

(1) We must constantly remind ourselves that *Scripture*, not our theologies, is our starting point.

(2) The ongoing work of the *Holy Spirit* instructs us in the truth. The same Holy Spirit speaks to persons in other cultures. They must therefore be allowed to interpret Scriptures for themselves. The work of the Spirit guards us from our cultural parochialisms.

(3) The *church* acts as a community of interpretation. Contextualization is ultimately the task of the church, rather than individuals or leaders. This corporate nature of the hermeneutical task helps

guard against the privatization of faith and from our individual misinterpretations of Scripture.

(4) A biblically based *theology* is essential. Central theological issues currently being discussed among evangelical scholars are Christology and the kingdom of God.

If any organization, movement, institution, or system is to enjoy any semblance of success or accomplishment it must structure principles of accountability within its framework of operation. This is no less true of religious institutions and movements.

Through the process of cross-cultural communication the mission evangelist engages in dialogue with persons of other cultures, hoping to share with them as well as learn from them. A deeper understanding and appreciation of other cultures fosters a spirit of openness to possibilities of contextualization or the communication of the gospel in the cultural context of the hearer.

Inculturation

Now we turn to a consideration of "inculturation," or as some might label it, "incarnation." In a simple definition, inculturation means uniting the gospel and the culture in marriage. This inevitably leads to the question, Is Christianity compatible with any and all cultures? To answer this question in the negative compromises the claim of John 3:16-17, "For God so loved the world that he gave his only Son, so that everyone who believes in him may not perish but may have eternal life. Indeed, God did not send the Son into the world to condemn the world, but in order that the world might be saved through him." And when one answers the question in the affirmative, one is in the company of those who can withhold the gospel from no one, because "all have sinned and fall short of the glory of God" (Rom. 3:23).

A significant value of engaging in dialogue is that of mutual accountability. When comparing biblical interpretation of a given scripture, it is not uncommon for new learnings to surface which may secure affirmation and confirmation for a solidly held belief by a person of a different culture. If we are honest, we will admit that a high percentage of our interpretation of Scripture is influenced by our culture, and we can see clearly the entrapment which this may produce. It is especially dangerous when allowed to run unabated, causing feelings of supremacy within one cultural group and disdain for members of another cultural group. In a pattern of intercultural (and also intracultural) dialogue, a system of checks and balances is developed which greatly reduces the chances of self-centered interpretation.

All things considered, it is unfair to assert that some of our practices are Christian, or scriptural, while others are cultural without being Christian. We must be very intentional in our efforts to ascertain the difference. It is an imposition of staggering weight to proclaim a Western or European Christ to an Eastern culture. Christ in his essence is sufficiently magnetic to draw all persons to himself. When what he says, and means, and does is properly and faithfully presented it will be culturally interpreted and adapted.

Indigenization is often deplored by the very ones who have themselves indigenized the gospel to serve their own selfish ends. Pluralism is a fact of our time, but too little is said or written about it that is complimentary. How can we overlook the record of Jesus in this regard? He gave status to those who had been forgotten and passed over, for example, women, lepers, and the poor. Pluralism is not a god, or an end in itself, as some would suggest. It does not necessarily breed relativism, which compromises the strength and vitality of the Christian witness. It can, if we allow it so to do, but if we truly understand who Christ is (and who he is not) it helps us to comprehend the depth, and scope, and variety of our humanity.

Inculturation (incarnation), to some extent, is practiced all over the world. Inculturation need not be uncritical adaptation. Inculturation can and does entail a prophetic critique of culture. Culturally sensitive Christians are called to continually challenge themselves and others to a life that becomes the gospel, to be in the world but not of the world.

The church in Japan is an excellent example of a small percentage of the populace giving faithful, consistent loyalty to Christ. It is clearly reminiscent of the stand taken by the early Christians. Here inculturation necessarily involves prophetic witness:

> Japanese Christians today try to emulate the examples of the early Christians. We believe that it is conceivable that a Christian can show greater loyalty to the state by disobeying—rather than obeying—its commands, especially when these are plainly contrary to Scripture.[8]

This is the testimony of Akiko Minato, who chairs the International Christian Studies Department of Tokyo Christian University.

The situation is basically the same in China. The Christian church is there, but the number of practicing Christians is very small, when compared to the overall population. The question which must be addressed is, "Can Christianity be embraced in China without integrating with the native culture?" And the answer seems at this time to be that "The possibility of a new era in Christianity in China and an appreciation of the Christian faith for the Chinese lie in the successful integration of Christianity with Chinese culture and in its efforts to co-exist and co-operate with Chinese tradition."[9]

I would argue that these national examples of Christian life and witness are hopeful signs of what can take place elsewhere. On the surface they may appear to be isolated incidents. It must also be noted that Buddhism and Shintoism in Japan, and Confucianism in China, have more adherents than Christianity in either place. But the possibility is there for all those religions to work together in a way that will signal unity amidst diversity. And that bodes well for Christianity, because if hermeneutical genocide can be avoided, abundant life in Jesus Christ can be offered and accepted.

The world for which Christ died is worthy of, and in need of, redemption. The world is larger than any one nation or continent; it is inclusive of all. Jesus Christ is the way to God and the ultimate revelation of God. Other faiths should be studied, and their disciples respected, but not at the expense of rejecting Christ. Ways and means must be discovered to proclaim Christ to the world without demeaning other cultures and without relativizing the Christian gospel. The kingdom of God is too important to exclude anyone or anything. Ultimately, it is God's call concerning how and when the Kingdom's final unveiling takes place. In the meantime, we are to be faithful and vigilant in our proclamation and our witness.

Let it be, dear Lord, let it be.

CHAPTER 13

The Global Gospel: A Response From an African Perspective

Arthur F. Kulah

THE MESSAGE OF UNIVERSAL GRACE entails a "globalization" of the Christian gospel. Once the issue of "globalization" is raised, the evangelistic and missiological issues of cross-cultural communication, contextualization, and inculturation confront us. Yet, what do we mean by "globalization"? Is it a process or a product? Is it a means or an end? A basic definition for this writer is an increased awareness among the nations and cultures of the world of a common existence and the consciousness that we are all members of the same household, community, or village. In essence, we are citizens of the global village.

In their book, *Megatrends 2000*, John Naisbit and Patricia Aburdene predict a global economic boom, global lifestyles, and cultural nationalism.[1] This globalization is made possible not only by improved telecommunications technology but by a *changed attitude* and disposition towards other nations and cultures of this global village.

Bishop Norris rightly recognizes the necessity and urgency of a *changed attitude* in a true globalization of evangelism and missiology. A changed attitude will eventuate in a more effective method of evangelizing. Such a method will facilitate the hearing of the gospel in various cultures and will help to shape and express the Christian faith in these same cultures in ways which are culturally appropriate.

The triad proposed by Bishop Norris—cross-cultural communication, contextualization, and inculturation—can actually be reduced to a dyad: cross-cultural communication and incarnation. In my recently published book, *Theological Education in Liberia: Problems and Opportunities*,[2] I argued that the term "Incarnation" was both inclusive and universal and that a "theology of the Incarnation" may be regarded as a "theology of the whole." The globalization of the gospel arises from an understanding and conviction that the Christian faith is truly a universal faith which requires the acceptance of a variety of cultural expressions while maintaining consistency with the theology and doctrines of the church. Incarnational theology includes contextualization or the attempt to witness to the gospel in radically changing economic, social, and political situations. Contextualization is not simply a matter of finding a new vocabulary. Contextualization is speaking the word of witness in the concrete socioeconomic and political context in which the church finds itself. The method of contextualization will always seek the dialectical tension between *identity* (i.e., consistency with the confessed tradition) and *relevancy* (i.e., speaking the concrete word in the concrete context).

Incarnational theology also includes inculturation or the cultural expression of the gospel in various ethnic traditions using symbols, proverbs, parables, and other media of communication particular to the given culture. In his widely acclaimed book, *Communicating Christ Cross-Culturally*,[3] David Hesselgrave discusses the dimensions of cross-cultural communication, which include understanding linguistic symbols, perceptions of the world, cognitive processes, behavioral patterns, social structures, and motivational sources.

Bishop Norris is right in pointing out that an acculturated Christian absolutism tends to produce anti-Christian behavior. What the early missionaries many times failed to realize is that they, too, contextualized the gospel. They contextualized the gospel in one culture and brought it culturally shaped into a different culture. In fairness it should be noted that many of the Protestant missionaries of the eighteenth and nineteenth centuries were not theologians and social scientists but were sincere people who were dedicated to their calling and the message of the "Great Commission." In many instances these eighteenth- and nineteenth-century missionaries were much more molded and shaped by Western cultural forces—such as the Renaissance, the Enlightenment, and the industrial revolution and its accompanying reordering of Western economic and political power—than they ever suspected. Their methods of witness to the gospel were often the only ones they had ever known, i.e., methods shaped and directed by the Second Great Awakening of the nineteenth century.

The strategy used by both Protestant and Catholic missionaries was to begin with a mission post which included a school, a hospital-clinic, a church, and an agricultural project. This construct resembled a Western parish set down in the midst of another culture. With language and cultural barriers, the missionaries began with the language they had and the culture they brought with them. Evangelization on one level was seen as effecting a cultural change. Hence, the criticism arose of "Western cultural imperialism."[4]

The problem at stake was not just "arrogance" and "a posture of superiority" but the resulting consequences of slavery, colonialism, and later neocolonialism. Let it nevertheless be said, the missionaries were sincere about their calling and should be credited for the desire and commitment to spread the gospel. There is no need constantly to point fingers and focus on the negative aspects of missionizing. Many of us who are beneficiaries of the missionary movement bear visible, physical witness to their labors.

A grappling with the issues and problems of cross-cultural communication can sensitize us to forms and practices of cultural oppression. At the same time, cross-cultural communication methods can provide for more effective hearing and receiving of the gospel. Cross-cultural communication is not monodirectional but properly proceeds in both directions. Bishop Norris rightly states learning about other cultures and experiencing them creates an appreciation and a deeper understanding of one's own culture.

One form of cross-cultural communication is interfaith dialogue. Such dialogue with other religions is crucial for mutual understanding and enriched self-understanding, but such dialogue should not compromise Christ's demand to "make disciples of all nations" (Matt. 28:19). According to the Christian tradition, it is God who took the initiative in Christ to enter human history by taking on human nature and human form. God became human to identify with humans.

Humanity is the object of God's action in Jesus Christ. At once, this is to raise the theological question of the relation of Christ and culture, since there is no humanity which is not cultural humanity. To claim, as Bishop Norris does, that "Christ is the object of every religious search" needs further clarification. If Christ is the object of every religious search, the method of Christian evangelization is determined by this. In his classic study, H. Richard Niebuhr provided a typology of five possible ways in which Christ interacts with culture.[5] Bishop Norris' suggestion seems to be closest to what Niebuhr called "the Christ of culture" type. Hesselgrave explains this type as basically claiming that Christian faith is not different from culture in kind but only in quality. People who take this position feel no tension between Christianity and other cultures because Christ is the truth in all religions. Bishop Norris rightly nuances this position to avoid minimizing the particularity of Jesus Christ.

Traces of this position can be seen in Scripture. In the Acts of the Apostles, Paul, while preaching in the city of Lystra, healed a man, and everyone thought Paul was a god. Paul, however, testified to the living God who "allowed all nations" to do what they wanted, "yet he has not left himself without a witness" (Acts 14:17). Jesus himself confirmed this earlier when he told his disciples "I have other sheep that do not belong to this fold. I must bring them also, and they will listen to my voice" (John 10:16). Even the prophet Amos showed that all nations are under God as he declared God's punishment on the nations for continuous transgression.

The ever-present danger with the "Christ of culture" position is that Christians can syncretize the gospel. Examples of this are found in early Christian Gnosticism and currently in some of the independent churches of Africa. We must guard against syncretizing because every culture stands under the mercy, judgment, and grace of Jesus Christ. In Liberia it is sometimes difficult to tell the difference between Christian and non-Christian practices in some of the independent African churches.

Another model of the Christ-culture interaction is what Niebuhr called "Christ, the Transformer of Culture" or the conversionist position. This position also holds a positive attitude toward culture but seeks to transform that culture by reinterpreting its symbols.

One must admit that morality and ethics seem to be the magnetic element of all religions, but Christological claims assert that the entire world is in need of God's saving grace. John Wesley distinguished between prevenient grace and saving grace; the latter is the grace that leads to and keeps the sinner in the kingdom of God. To claim that all religions already know Christ is to stop at prevenient grace. To argue that Christ is the "transformer" of culture is to affirm the Incarnation, that God came searching for lost humanity. Culture, whatever culture, can be redeemed and transformed.

The church cannot and must not neglect its evangelistic task. The church today is finding new and diverse ways to be in ministry. When social services are rendered, such action is always infused with the conviction that God's redemptive action in Jesus Christ entails such ministry. Such ministry is expressive of God's love for humankind in Jesus Christ. It is never a matter of producing "rice-Christians." The church cannot give up the preaching of the word and the serving of tables. No, never. The center of our message is Jesus Christ, crucified and resurrected, the universal Lord of all cultures and, hence, the "Transformer" of all of human life.

Incarnational Theology and Africa

Since the 1960s the church in Africa has begun a journey to make Christianity more relevant and significant, reflecting the African culture and the socioeconomic realities on the continent. At some point in this journey, the church in Africa identified with movements in Latin America and accepted various forms of liberation theology. African theologians also read and studied black theology expressive of black persons in the United States struggling for their integrity as a people. Over a period of time, however, African leaders have come to realize that some expressions of liberation theology were being carried to extremes, calling for the church to support and even participate in violent revolutionary activities. This has forced the church in Africa to rethink its position and stance.

Beginning in the 1990s, the All-Africa Conference of Churches initiated what is now known as the "Theology of Reconstruction."[6] Finding theological justification in the prophecy of Nehemiah, by which the people of Jerusalem were organized to rebuild the city (Nehemiah 2:17), Africans were urged "to do whatever they can wherever they are."[7]

The challenges facing the church in Africa are great. In response to those challenges, I have recently suggested that contemporary theological education in Liberia be restructured not only to reflect traditional Christian training but also to address the need of pastors to understand popular religious forms such as witchcraft, dreams, and human sacrifices. In addition, I call for an "equilibrium which enables universality and particularity, adaptation and conservation, to support each other for effective ministries for the church of Jesus Christ."[8]

For Western church leaders to experience the global nature of the gospel, they must possess at least a basic understanding of worldviews, cognitive processes, and symbolic expressions of other cultures. Such cross-cultural learning is essential today because we are living in a new situation where the issue is not just how to communicate the faith in a non-Western culture. Non-Western cultures and churches are now witnessing in the cultural West.

The globalization of the gospel is not an option but an opportunity which must be utilized through careful reflection, analysis, and application. The benefits are many, among which are deeper appreciation of cultures, a reliance on the Holy Spirit to facilitate the discernment process, new means of articulating and expressing the gospel message, and a sense of oneness among Christians.

In this process, it is instructive to recognize the mistakes of the past but not dwell on them. We need to move forward! The verbal proclamation of the gospel must never ever be deemphasized, but rather it should take precedence over visual and social expressions of the gospel. A mutual exchange of pastors and church leaders could reveal to all peoples that no matter what culture is one's own, the gospel of Jesus Christ is universal and transcultural. It is the task of the church to make this audible and visible.

APPENDIX

"God's Gracious Love Affair":
A Sermon on Isaiah 43:1-4

Joseph H. Yeakel

AND NOW, O GOD, either through me or in spite of me, speak to your people. Grant all of us ears to hear what your Spirit is saying to the church and churches, and especially to the community gathered in this sanctuary on this beautiful spring morning. And having heard, then grant to each of us grace, and faith, and courage to be, and to do, what you would yet have of us, for we pray in the name of Jesus the Christ, our Lord. *Amen.*

◆ ◆ ◆

In all honesty, I found this preaching assignment a rather difficult one. I didn't quite know how to get ready for this. After all, if the Consultation spent four days explicating evangelism and evangelization in depth, with the responders and the discussions and all that went with it, is there anything left to be said? On the other hand, I recognize that the vast majority of those here this morning were not present throughout the Consultation and so we were coming to this time of worship without the Consultation's orientation. How does one gather up these two extremes and bring them together in a time of worship?

I don't know about you, but does your mind ever have a mind of its own? Have you ever experienced those moments when you think that you've got things in hand and you're headed in a certain direction and all of a sudden, your mind takes over and goes in a different direction? Is that an uncommon experience or something I should worry about? Because try as I did in preparing for this occasion, and I tried multiple times, I found myself being brought back to an incident that took place in my life and the lives of loved ones and friends not too long ago.

On the 28th of December past, there was a birth in the lives of a family in the Baltimore-Washington Conference. A birth that in and of itself was truly miraculous. A birth that was hard to believe would ever take place.

The mother, shortly after being married to the father, was taken ill with an unusual form of abdominal cancer which required the physicians and surgeons to enter her body and literally wash the abdomen with chemicals, not once, not twice, but multiple times. First imagine the destruction that takes place during such extreme chemotherapy. I am sure you can imagine it for yourselves. That series of events is hard to describe.

We despaired for her life time and again, and yet the fight and determination on her part and the skill of the medical community managed to bring her through. She told me she told her doctor, "I suppose even though I survived all of this, I'll never be a mother." He didn't answer the question directly. The conversations along this line continued and sometime later there was just a hint that there might be a possibility of giving birth.

With their determination and the help of medical science, she did become pregnant. But early on, she miscarried. Then in the grace of God, she became pregnant again and carried the baby almost to term. He arrived on the scene December 28, 1994. He lived six days. It was necessary to take him to another hospital where they could provide the special care that he needed, including several heart surgeries. How do you perform surgery on the heart of a child so small? Ultimately, he didn't survive.

They invited me to share in the memorial celebration. You don't say "no" to those invitations, but you do say to yourself "now that I've said yes, what do I say?" Is there a word of God for that moment? Given what's happened, given the setting, given all that I've shared with you—and I've only touched the surface—you can get a sense of what was going in the life of that family.

In my devotional life, the lectionary readings were leading me through the words of Isaiah. I would never have expected to find a word for this occasion in the midst of the prophet's writings, but there it was. I asked to have it read this morning—this word to a people in the second and third generations as "prisoners of war," "displaced persons" experiencing the worst of times, and asking if there is nothing that God has to say to us, or even worse, has God simply forgotten us? Isaiah responds with God's message for them:

> Thus says the LORD, he who created you, O Jacob,
>   he who formed you, O Israel:
> Do not fear, for I have redeemed you;
>   I have called you by name, you are mine.
> When you pass through the waters, I will be with you;
>   and through the rivers, they shall not overwhelm you;
> when you walk through fire you shall not be burned,
>   and the flame shall not consume you.
> For I am the LORD your God, the Holy One of Israel,
>   your Savior....
> Because you are precious in my sight,
>   and honored, and I love you. (Isaiah 43:1-4)

I have called you by name, you are mine. This is God's gracious love affair with us! Isn't this exactly what God has done in your life and mine?

We shouldn't be surprised, should we? God's gracious love affair does surprise us. After all, we've all referred to that verse in John's gospel, "for God so loved the world," haven't we? I don't know when I learned to say that God loved the world. But what I really learned was that God loved the church. My church was First Church back home; there was a Second Church in the town. We knew God loved First Church; we weren't quite so sure about God and Second Church and in our little coal-mining town in Pennsylvania, I also learned that God didn't love the Roman Catholic Church, the reason for this not being very clear. I had to learn that verse all over again—that God loved the world. God's love is an inclusive love—not an exclusive love. I have called you by name, you are mine. I love you.

Love is "something else." When I graduated from seminary, my wife Lois was pregnant. We had a daughter at the time, and we were now expecting another addition to our family. Seminary graduation was in May and Annual Conference met in October and I had a growing family to support.

I was lucky enough to be employed as the grounds manager at our camp. That meant that I was taking my graduate degree in plumbing. (Do you know how many flushes go with the summer camp program?) At any rate, there we were, Lois and I and Claudia, living in a very small cottage on the grounds of the camp that summer. The time for our second child to be born was getting closer and closer.

We were sitting on the porch of the cottage one night, and I turned to Lois and said, "You know, honey, I'm scared." She says she doesn't remember this, but I know what she said. She said "I don't know why you're scared—you're not going to have this baby."

But I really was scared. The reason was quite simple. When Claudia came into our lives, that was an experience that I'll never forget. I never loved a person quite like I loved her. I'm sure Lois has understood that I wasn't comparing my love for her and my love for Claudia, but to have a daughter, to have a child of our own, to love that child—well, what made me scared was that now we were going to have another child. How was I going to divide that love? How could I take what I've given all to Claudia and divide it up with somebody else? But, I was convinced I was going to have to divide that love somehow.

I don't know how we concluded the conversation, but within a couple of weeks Doug arrived, and I learned about that business of love which really is "something else." I never had to divide my love. What I discovered was that the capacity to love was doubled. (And it's a good thing the capacity was doubled, because three more children came after Doug.)

I called you by name, you're mine, and I love you. There's always room for one more. That's what Paul was saying to the church at Corinth. When anyone is in Christ, when anyone knows and responds to God's gracious love, then that person is a new creation. The old is gone, it's like being born again. There's always room in love for one more.

Recently a delegation from the General Board of Church and Society had the opportunity to visit The Methodist Church of Cuba and learn about its life and ministry and witness over many years and in difficult times. In a conversation with Bishop Joel Ajo, the bishop of The Methodist Church of Cuba, they discussed what it was that had really gotten hold of the lives of the people under such circumstances. He referred to his experience of being jailed for two and a half years in the mid-1970s for being a minister of the church:

> I have to be very honest with you, when this first happened, I lost all sense of faith. I was angry; I withdrew; I rebelled; I didn't want any part of anything or anybody and I could feel life going out of me. And then, when I came to the place where I began to accept my

relationship with my fellow prisoners and I began to reach out to them.... I found myself bonding with them in the place where we were.

He went on to say that it was that experience of bonding with others that "restored my own life and has supported me all of these years since."

God was in Christ bonding with us; reconciling the world to himself. In his Cotton Patch version of 2 Cor. 5:19, Clarence Jordan says "God was in Christ hugging the world to himself and gives us, gives *us*, the ministry of hugging the world in God's name." What a gracious love affair: bonded, hugged, reconciled. For the God who so loves the world, and whose love includes us, wills to love that world through us.

For me, this is the heart and essence of evangelism. Good news! May it be so.

Contributors

THE FOUNDATION FOR EVANGELISM thanks the following bishops of The United Methodist Church for allowing the essays that they prepared for presentation to the Consultation on Theology and Evangelism to be edited for publication in this volume.

George W. Bashore, Bishop of the Pittsburgh Area.

Bruce P. Blake, Bishop of the Dallas Area.

Edwin C. Boulton, Bishop of the East Ohio Area.

Kenneth L. Carder, Bishop of the Nashville Area.

R. Sheldon Duecker, Bishop of the Chicago Area.

Elias G. Galvan, Bishop of the Phoenix Area.

Neil L. Irons, Bishop of the New Jersey Area.

Hae-Jong Kim, Bishop of the New York West Area.

Arthur F. Kulah, Bishop of the Liberia Area.

Ruediger R. Minor, Bishop of the Eurasia Area.

Alfred L. Norris, Bishop of the Northwest Texas-New Mexico Area.

Ann B. Sherer, Bishop of the Missouri Area.

Woodie W. White, Bishop of the Indiana Area.

Richard B. Wilke, Bishop of the Arkansas Area.

Joseph H. Yeakel, Bishop of the Washington Area.

Respondents

THE FOUNDATION FOR EVANGELISM acknowledges with gratitude that the following individuals served as respondents to the major presentations at the Consultation on Theology and Evangelism, and sincerely regrets that considerations of space prohibit the inclusion of their responses in this volume.

W. Stephen Gunter, Arthur J. Moore Associate Professor of Evangelism, Candler School of Theology, Emory University, Atlanta, Georgia.

Carolyn E. Johnson, President, The United Methodist Women; Professor of African-American Studies, Purdue University, West Lafayette, Indiana.

Henry H. Knight III, E. Stanley Jones Professor of Evangelism, Saint Paul School of Theology, Kansas City, Missouri.

David J. Lawson, Bishop of the Illinois Area.

James K. Mathews, retired bishop, Washington, D.C.

Robert J. Stamps, Senior Pastor, Clarendon United Methodist Church, Arlington, Virginia.

K. James Stein, Jubilee Professor of Church History, Garrett-Evangelical Theological Seminary, Evanston, Illinois.

Robert K. Swanson, Director, Evangelism Ministries, General Board of Discipleship, Nashville, Tennessee.

Sondra Ely Wheeler, Associate Professor of Christian Ethics, Wesley Theological Seminary, Washington, D.C.

Abbreviations

Journal	*The Journal of the Rev. John Wesley, A.M.*, edited by Nehemiah Curnock, 8 volumes (London: Epworth Press, 1909–1916).
Letters	*The Letters of the Rev. John Wesley, A.M.*, edited by John Telford, 8 volumes (London: Epworth Press, 1931).
Works	*The Works of John Wesley*, begun as "The Oxford Edition of *The Works of John Wesley*" (Oxford: Clarendon Press, 1975–1983); continued as "The Bicentennial Edition of *The Works of John Wesley*" (Nashville: Abingdon Press, 1984—); 15 of 35 volumes published to date.
Works (J)	*The Works of the Rev. John Wesley, M.A.*, edited by Thomas Jackson, 3rd edition, 14 volumes (London: Wesleyan Methodist Book Room, 1872; reprinted Grand Rapids: Baker Book House, 1979).

Notes

Notes to Introduction

1. Article by E. S. James in *The Methodist Magazine and Quarterly Review*, vol. 22, New Series, vol. XI (1840). Quoted by David C. Shipley in *The Ministry in the Methodist Heritage* (Nashville: Department of Ministerial Education, 1960), 28.

2. *In Defense of Creation* (Nashville: Graded Press, 1986).

3. *Vital Congregations/Faithful Disciples* (Nashville: Graded Press, 1990).

4. P. T. Forsyth, *The Cruciality of the Cross* (London: Independent Press, 1919).

Notes to Chapter 1

1. Victor Paul Furnish, *Jesus According to Paul* (Cambridge: Cambridge University Press, 1993), 67.
2. Ludwig Köhler, *Old Testament Theology* (Philadelphia: Westminster Press, 1953), 87.
3. Thomas F. Torrance, *The Mediation of Christ* (Grand Rapids: Wm. B. Eerdmans, 1983), 18.
4. Klaus Koch, *The Prophets*, 2 vols. (Philadelphia: Fortress Press, 1984), 2:184.
5. Furnish, *Jesus According to Paul*, 68.
6. Leander E. Keck, *Paul and His Letters* (Philadelphia: Fortress Press, 1979), 50.

Notes to Chapter 2

1. Albert C. Outler, *Evangelism in the Wesleyan Spirit* (Nashville: Tidings, 1971), 76.
2. Leander E. Keck, *The Church Confident* (Nashville: Abingdon Press, 1993), 22.
3. "Dead End for the Mainline," *Newsweek* (August 9, 1993), 42–48.
4. Loren B. Mead, *The Once and Future Church* (Washington, DC: Alban Institute, 1991), 3.
5. Leonard Sweet, "The Martha Memorial" (unpublished paper delivered in Atlanta, Georgia, in February, 1989).
6. Wade Clark Roof, "The Third Disestablishment and Beyond," in *Mainstream Protestantism in the Twentieth Century: Its Problems and Prospects*, ed. Dorothy C. Bass, Benton Johnson, and Wade Clark Roof (Louisville: Commission on Theological Education, Presbyterian Church USA, 1990), 29, 30.
7. Wesley, "Salvation by Faith," *Works*, 1:117–18.
8. Ben Witherington, III, "*Praeparatio Evangelii*: Theological Roots of Wesley's View of Evangelism," in *Theology and Evangelism in the Wesleyan Heritage*, ed. James C. Logan (Nashville: Kingswood Books, 1994), 210.
9. Wesley, "The Scripture Way of Salvation," *Works*, 2:156–57.
10. Wesley, "Working Out Our Own Salvation," *Works*, 3:203.
11. Ibid.
12. David Lowes Watson, "The Making of Disciples in the Methodist Tradition" (unpublished paper delivered in Atlanta, Georgia, in March, 1989), 6.
13. Outler, *Evangelism*, 46.
14. Watson, "The Making of Disciples," 6.
15. Wesley, "The Scripture Way of Salvation," *Works*, 2:157.

16. David Lowes Watson, *The Early Methodist Class Meeting* (Nashville: Discipleship Resources, 1985), 64.
17. Wesley, "The Scripture Way of Salvation," *Works*, 2:158.
18. Ibid., 2:161.
19. Leonard Sweet, *FaithQuakes* (Nashville: Abingdon Press, 1994), 87.
20. Ibid., 71.
21. Wesley, "Justification by Faith," *Works*, 1:182.
22. Outler, *Evangelism*, 38.
23. Wesley, "On God's Vineyard," *Works*, 3:507.
24. Wesley, "Plain Account of Christian Perfection," *Works* (J), 11:394.
25. Wesley, "The Scripture Way of Salvation," *Works*, 2:156.
26. Ibid., 2:165.
27. Theodore W. Jennings, Jr., "Conversion and Discipleship in Wesley's Thought," (unpublished paper delivered in Atlanta, Georgia, in February, 1989), 4.
28. Wesley, *Works*, 21:299.
29. Richard Heitzenrater, *Mirror and Memory: Reflections on Early Methodism* (Nashville: Kingswood Books, 1989), 147.
30. Watson, *The Early Methodist Class Meeting*, 71.
31. James C. Logan, "The Evangelical Imperative: A Wesleyan Perspective" in *Theology and Evangelism in the Wesleyan Heritage*, ed. James C. Logan (Nashville: Kingswood Books, 1994), 18.
32. Heitzenrater, *Mirror and Memory*, 163.
33. Logan, "The Evangelical Imperative," 18.
34. Heitzenrater, *Memory and Mirror*, 132.
35. Outler, *Evangelism*, 55.
36. Watson, *The Early Methodist Class Meeting*, 71.
37. Julia Wedgewood, *John Wesley and the Evangelical Reaction of the Eighteenth Century* (London: Macmillan, 1870), 156–57; quoted in Watson, *The Early Methodist Class Meeting*, 74.
38. Wesley, "A Plain Account of the People Called Methodists," *Works*, 9:256.
39. Ibid.
40. Ibid.
41. Wesley, "The Nature, Design and General Rules of the United Societies," *Works*, 9:70.
42. Wesley, *Works*, 21:227.
43. Wesley, *Works*, 21:226.
44. Watson, *The Early Methodist Class Meeting*, 132.
45. Ibid., 116.
46. Wesley, *Works*, 21:26.
47. Outler, *Evangelism*, 55.
48. Watson, *The Early Methodist Class Meeting*, 94.
49. Wesley, "Justification by Faith," *Works*, 1:187; italics in original.

50. Wesley, "The Scripture Way of Salvation," *Works*, 2:158.
51. Sweet, *FaithQuakes*, 64.
52. Logan, "The Evangelical Imperative," 20.
53. *Newsweek* (November 28, 1994), 53.

Notes to Chapter 3

1. J. Steven O'Malley, "The Otterbeins: Men of Two Worlds," *Methodist History*, 15/1 (October 1976), 7, 8.
2. *The Heidelberg Catechism* (Philadelphia: United Church Press, 1963), 9–24.
3. O'Malley, "The Otterbeins," 12.
4. Ibid., 13.
5. Philip William Otterbein, "*Die Heilbringende Menschwerdung Und Der Herrliche Sieg Jesu Christi Ueber Den Teufel Und Tod.*" Sermon translated by Ehrhardt Lang (Germantown: Christoph Sauer, 1763); available through United Theological Seminary, Dayton, Ohio.
6. P. B. Gibble, *History of the East Pennsylvania Conference of the United Brethren in Christ* (Dayton: Otterbein Press, 1951), 9.
7. J. Steven O'Malley, *The Otterbeins: The Postlude of Pietism* (Ph.D. dissertation, Drew University, 1970), 457.
8. Abraham W. Sangrey, *Martin Boehm*, (Ephrate, PA: Science Press, 1976), 9–11.
9. Raymond W. Albright, *A History of the Evangelical Church* (Harrisburg, PA: The Evangelical Press, 1956), 34–35.
10. Raymond M. Veh, "John Seybert—Symbol of a Passion" (unpublished paper presented to the Historical Society of the Wisconsin Conference, U.M. Church, October 4, 1986).
11. As quoted in Veh, "John Seybert."
12. James I. Good, *The Heidelberg Catechism in Its Newest Light* (Philadelphia: Reformed Church, 1914), 295–96.
13. Paul H. Eller, *These Evangelical United Brethren* (Dayton, OH: Otterbein Press, 1950), 29–31.
14. Johann Lawrence, *Die Kirchengeschichte der Vereinigten Brüder in Christo* (Dayton, OH: Schulz, 1871).
15. Arthur C. Core, *Philip William Otterbein: Pastor, Ecumenist* (Dayton, OH: Board of Publication, 1968), 60.
16. *The Heidelberg Catechism*, 9.

Notes to Chapter 4

1. Douglas W. Johnson, *Vitality Means Church Growth* (Nashville: Abingdon Press, 1989), 116.

2. Norman Shawchuck, *Marketing for Congregations* (Nashville: Abingdon Press, 1992), 83–86.
3. Howard Snyder, *Liberating the Church* (Downers Grove, IL: InterVarsity Press, 1983), 11.
4. Henry H. Knight, III, "The Baptismal Shaping of Christian Lives," *Doxology* 7 (1990), 17.
5. George G. Hunter, III, *How to Reach Secular People* (Nashville: Abingdon Press, 1992), 110.
6. Barbara Wendland, *Connections* 27 (January 1995), 1.
7. Elton Trueblood, *The Incendiary Fellowship* (New York: Harper & Row, 1967), 26.
8. Ibid., 111.
9. Johnson, *Vitality Means Church Growth*, 18
10. Eddie H. Fox and George E. Morris, *Faith-Sharing* (Nashville: Discipleship Resources, 1986), 15.
11. Eddie H. Fox and George E. Morris, *Let the Redeemed of the Lord Say So!* (Nashville: Abingdon Press, 1991), 161–62.
12. Hunter, *How to Reach Secular People*, 20.
13. Fox and Morris, *Faith-Sharing*, 74.
14. Walter Brueggemann, *Biblical Perspectives on Evangelism* (Nashville: Abingdon Press, 1993), 123.
15. James Adams, *So You Can't Stand Evangelism?* (Cambridge: Cowley Publishing, 1994), 16.
16. George Barna, *User Friendly Churches* (Ventura: Regal Books, 1991), 100.
17. Carl S. Dudley and Douglas A. Walrath, *Developing Your Small Church's Potential* (Valley Forge: Judson Press, 1988).
18. Edwin Friedman, *Generation to Generation: Family Process in Church and Synagogue* (New York: Guilford Press, 1985).
19. Loren Mead, *The Once and Future Church* (Washington, DC: Alban Institute, 1991).
20. Hunter, *How To Reach Secular People*.
21. Tex Sample, *Hard Living People and Mainstream Christians* (Nashville: Abingdon Press, 1993).
22. Adams, *So You Can't Stand Evangelism?*, 185.

Notes to Chapter 5

1. Kenneth L. Carder, "Proclaiming the Gospel of Grace," in *Theology and Evangelism in the Wesleyan Heritage*, ed. James C. Logan (Nashville: Kingswood Books, 1994), 91. See Wesley's sermon, "Causes of the Inefficacy of Christianity," *Works*, 4:96.
2. George G. Hunter, III, *To Spread the Gospel* (Nashville: Abingdon Press, 1987), 39–62.

3. See Halford E. Luccock, *Endless Line of Splendor*, rev. ed. (Evanston: Commission on Promotion and Cultivation of the Methodist Church, 1964), 66–67.
4. Mortimer Arias, *The Great Commission: Biblical Models for Evangelism* (Nashville: Abingdon Press, 1992).
5. Dietrich Bonhoeffer, *The Cost of Discipleship* (New York: Macmillan, 1963), 29.
6. Leander E. Keck, "What Makes Romans Tick?" (unpublished essay).
7. Pope John Paul II, *Crossing the Threshold of Hope* (New York: Alfred A. Knopf, 1994), 58.
8. E. Stanley Jones, *Christian Maturity* (Nashville: Abingdon Press, 1957), 185.
9. Pope John Paul II, *Crossing the Threshold of Hope*, 117.
10. Wesley, *Letters*, 3:229 (to Dorothy Furly, September 25, 1757).
11. Carder, "Proclaiming the Gospel of Grace," 91.

Notes to Chapter 6

1. Lesslie Newbigin, in *The Gospel in a Pluralist Society* (Grand Rapids: Wm. B. Eerdmans, 1989), deals with this issue in a very helpful way.
2. *Grace Upon Grace: The Mission Statement of The United Methodist Church* (Nashville: Graded Press, 1990).

Notes to Chapter 7

1. Anders Nygren, *Agape and Eros* (Philadelphia: Westminster Press, 1953).
2. George G. Hunter, III, *The Contagious Congregation: Frontiers in Evangelism and Church Growth* (Nashville: Abingdon Press, 1979).
3. Robert Wuthnow, *Christianity in the Twenty-First Century: Reflections on the Challenges Ahead* (New York: Oxford University Press, 1993).
4. Robert Bellah, et al., *Habits of the Heart: Individualism and Commitment in American Life* (Berkeley: University of California Press, 1985).
5. Donald A. McGavran, *Understanding Church Growth*, (Grand Rapids: Wm. B. Eerdmans, 1980).
6. Stanley Hauerwas and William H. Willimon, *Resident Aliens: Life in the Christian Colony* (Nashville: Abingdon Press, 1990), 51–52.
7. Loren Mead, *The Once and Future Church* (Washington, DC: Alban Institute, 1991), 7–13.
8. Leander E. Keck, *The Church Confident* (Nashville: Abingdon Press, 1993), 65–67.

Notes to Chapter 8

1. Orlando Costas, *Liberating News: A Theology of Contextual Evangelism* (Grand Rapids: Wm. B. Eerdmans, 1989), 21.
2. Ibid., 23.
3. Ibid., 23.
4. E. Stanley Jones, *Christ of the Round Table* (Nashville: Abingdon Press, 1928).
5. See John Koenig, *New Testament Hospitality: Partnership with Strangers as Promise and Mission* (Philadelphia: Fortress Press, 1985). For a sociological treatment sensitive to issues of spirituality, see Parker J. Palmer, *Company of Strangers: Christians and the Renewal of America's Public Life* (New York: Crossroad, 1991). For a challenging treatment of hospitality as a central theological, liturgical, and evangelistic notion, see Patrick R. Keifert, *Welcoming the Stranger: A Public Theology of Worship and Evangelism* (Minneapolis: Fortress Press, 1992).
6. Henri Nouwen, *Reaching Out: Three Movements of the Spiritual Life* (Garden City, NY: Doubleday & Co., 1975).
7. See Howard Mellor's treatment, "Evangelism and Religious Pluralism in the Wesleyan Heritage," in *Theology and Evangelism in the Wesleyan Heritage*, ed. James C. Logan (Nashville: Kingswood Books, 1994), 123.
8. Faith Popcorn, *Popcorn Report: Faith Popcorn on the Future of Your Company, Your World, Your Life* (San Francisco: Harper & Row, 1992).
9. Leonard Sweet, *FaithQuakes* (Nashville: Abingdon Press, 1994), 21.
10. Mortimer Arias, "Centripetal Mission or Evangelization by Hospitality," *Missiology* 11 (January 1982), 69–82.

Notes to Chapter 9

1. This story, told by many people, has been recorded among others by Dorothee Sölle, *Die Wahrheit ist konkret* (Olten, Freiburg: Walter-Verlag, 1968).
2. Harvey Cox, *The Secular City* (New York: Macmillan, 1965).
3. Immanuel Kant, "What Is Enlightenment?" (1784), in *The Enlightenment: A Comprehensive Anthology*, ed. Peter Gay (New York: Simon and Schuster, 1973), 384–89.
4. George G. Hunter III, *How to Reach Secular People* (Nashville: Abingdon Press, 1992), 21–39.
5. Ibid., 23.
6. Dietrich Bonhoeffer, *Letters and Papers from Prison*, enlarged edition, ed. Eberhard Bethge (New York: MacMillan, 1971).
7. The Marxist philosopher Ernst Bloch in his book, *Atheism in Christianity: The Religion of the Exodus and the Kingdom* (New York: Herder

and Herder, 1979), develops this similarity of Christianity and atheism in the dialectical sentence: "Only a Christian can be an atheist, only an atheist can be a Christian."

8. R. Thaut, "Säkularismus, –isierung, –isation," in *Evangelisches Gemeindelexicon* (Wuppertal: R. Brockhaus Verlag, 1978), 450; translation by the author.

9. See Dietrich Bonhoeffer's notion of "world come of age" in *Letters and Papers from Prison*. On the relation between Christian faith and secularization in Friedrich Gogarten's theology see especially two of his books: *The Reality of Faith* (Philadelphia: Westminster Press, 1959), and *The Fate and Hope of the Modern Era* (Philadelphia: Westminster Press, 1968).

10. Thaut, "Säkularismus," 450.

11. An unpublished paper read before German church workers, March 1994.

12. Ulrich Zwingli, *Commentary on True and False Religion* (Durham, NC: Labyrinth Press, 1918).

13. Eberhard Jüngel, "Säkularisierung—Theologische Anmerkunger zum Begriff einer weltlichen Welt," in *Christliche Freiheit in Dienst am Menschen. Zum 80. Geburtstag vom Martin Niemöller* (Frankfurt am Main: O. Lembeck, 1972), 163–68.

14. From Martin Luther's 1533 sermon on the creed as quoted in Jüngel, "Säkularisierung," 165; translation by the author.

15. G. Howard Mellor, "Evangelism and Religious Pluralism in the Wesleyan Heritage," in *Theology and Evangelism in the Wesleyan Heritage*, ed. James C. Logan (Nashville: Kingswood Books, 1994), 109–126.

16. Ibid., 124ff.

Notes to Chapter 10

1. Ben Wattenberg, *The Good News Is the Bad News Is Wrong* (New York: Simon and Schuster, 1984).

2. H. Eddie Fox and George E. Morris, *Faith-Sharing* (Nashville: Discipleship Resources, 1966).

3. Ibid., 1.

4. E. Stanley Jones, *A Song of Ascents: A Spiritual Autobiography* (Nashville: Abingdon Press, 1968), 385–86.

5. Charles Dickens, *A Tale of Two Cities* (New York: Macmillan, 1926), 1.

6. George F. MacLeod, *Only One Way Left: Church Prospect* (Glasgow: Iona Community, 1956), 164.

7. Wesley, *Works*, 19:46 (Journal for April 1, 1739; italics in original).

8. Ibid.; italics in original.

9. Wesley, "The Signs of the Times," *Works*, 2:527.

10. Kenneth Carder, "Proclaiming the Gospel of Grace," in *Theology and Evangelism in the Wesleyan Heritage*, ed. James C. Logan (Nashville: Kingswood Books, 1994), 92.

11. Howard F. Masher, *A Stranger in the Kingdom* (New York: Doubleday, 1989).

12. Robert Wuthnow, *God and Mammon in America* (New York: The Free Press, 1994), 9.

13. L. Harold DeWolf, *The Enduring Message of the Bible* (New York: Harper and Row, 1960), 116.

14. Leonard Sweet, *FaithQuakes* (Nashville: Abingdon Press, 1994), 27.

Notes to Chapter 11

1. See the perceptive analysis of Enlightenment epistemology in Lesslie Newbigin, *The Gospel in a Pluralist Society* (Grand Rapids: Wm. B. Eerdmans, 1989), 14–38.

2. Quoted in Clarence C. Goen, "Ecclesiocracy Without Ecclesiology," in *Prophetic Memory for the Contemporary Church: Collected Writings of C. C. Goen*, ed. Mark S. Burrows (Barre, VT: Northlight Studio Press, 1991), 274.

3. D. T. Niles, "The Christian Claim for the Finality of Christ," in *The Finality of Christ*, ed. Dow Kirkpatrick (Nashville: Abingdon Press, 1966), 14.

4. The church's affirmation of the finality of Christ is crucial for the church's mission and evangelism. The issue is currently pressing not only because of religious pluralism (this has always been a universal phenomenon) but also because of voices within the church today calling for a theology of religious pluralism which relativizes and "de-norms" the Christian claim of the finality of Christ. See John Hick and Paul F. Knitter, eds., *The Myth of Christian Uniqueness: Towards a Pluralistic Theology of Religions* (Maryknoll, NY: Orbis Books, 1987). Contemporary theological efforts to address this issue from a normative stance include Carl E. Braaten, *No Other Gospel!* (Minneapolis: Fortress Press, 1992), and Harold A. Netland, *Dissonant Voices: Religious Pluralism and the Question of Truth* (Grand Rapids: Wm. B. Eerdmans, 1991).

5. Goen, "Ecclesiocracy Without Ecclesiology," 266.

6. Leander E. Keck, *The Church Confident* (Nashville: Abingdon Press, 1993), 57.

Notes to Chapter 12

1. See the varying forms of the "Great Commission" in Matthew 28:16-20, Mark 16:14-18, Luke 24:36-49, and John 20:19-23; cf. Acts 1:6-8.

2. Mortimer Arias and Alan Johnson, *The Great Commission: Biblical Models for Evangelism* (Nashville: Abingdon Press, 1992), 16.

3. Dana Rodenbaugh, "Unique Parliament of World Religions Celebrate Diversity," *National Catholic Reporter* (17 September 1993), 3.

4. Duane Elmer, *Cross-Cultural Conflict* (Downers Grove: InterVarsity Press, 1993), 24.

5. Marcus Bach, *Major Religions of the World* (Nashville: The Graded Press, 1959), 13–14.

6. Richard Mouw, "Preaching Christ or Packaging Jesus," *Christianity Today* (11 February 1991), 30.

7. Paul G. Hiebert, "Checks Against Syncretism," *Christianity Today* (11 February 1991), 39–40.

8. Akiko Minato, "The Japanese Church's Most Critical Issue," *Christianity Today* (8 April 1991), 30.

9. Xinghong Yao, "Success or Failure? Christianity in China," *History Today* (September 1994), 9–10.

Notes to Chapter 13

1. John Naisbit and Patricia Aburdene, *Megatrends 2000* (New York: Morrow, 1990).

2. Arthur F. Kulah, *Theological Education in Liberia: Problems and Opportunities* (Lithonia, GA: SCP/Third World Publishing House, 1994), 59.

3. David Hesselgrave, *Communicating Christ Cross-Culturally* (Grand Rapids: Zondervan Publishing House, 1978), 8–11.

4. Ross E. Dunn, et al., *Links Across Time and Place* (Chicago: McDougal, Littell & Company, 1990), 558.

5. H. Richard Niebuhr, *Christ and Culture* (New York: Harper & Row, 1956).

6. José Chipenda, et al., *The Church of Africa: Towards a Theology of Reconstruction* (Nairobi: All-Africa Conference of Churches, 1991).

7. José Chipenda, AACC Secretary-General, in a lecture to the Gbarnga School of Theology, Monrovia, Liberia, 7 July 1994.

8. Kulah, *Theological Education in Liberia*, 41.